# What Others Are Saying About This Book

"A book by the master of libertarian persuasion. This is modeled after the dozens of seminars and personal training sessions he's conducted — all leading to rave reviews from people who have used his techniques with great success."
—**Harry Browne**, author, *How I Found Freedom In An Unfree World*

"I've read *Secrets of Libertarian Persuasion* from cover to cover, and I congratulate you on a fine and valuable book. I hope it spreads — and sells — widely among the people who are, often helplessly, attempting to spread the message of freedom."
—**Barbara Branden**, author, *The Passion of Ayn Rand*

"Libertarian persuasion at its most eloquent and powerful. *Secrets* can help you become a superstar persuader for the cause of Liberty. This is the best book on overall persuasion — not just libertarian — I've ever read. Own it and watch your communication abilities, and most likely your income, grow and grow."
—**Bob Burg**, author, *Endless Referrals*

"*Secrets of Libertarian Persuasion* is filled with one unique insight after another on how to think and talk about liberty. Michael's 'Weight Watcher's Test' for evaluating politicians in itself is worth more than the meager price of the book."
—**Dr. Michael Edelstein**, psychologist, author, *Three Minute Therapy*

"Too many libertarians do all the wrong things to promote freedom. *Secrets of Libertarian Persuasion* tells them all the right ways. It's based on common sense, good science, and good psychology. Every serious libertarian needs to read this invaluable book."
—**Sharon Presley**, Ph.D., psychologist, co-founder, Laissez Faire Books

"Whatever you think of politics, I think you should get this book. *Secrets of Libertarian Persuasion* contains many short but powerful methods of persuasion. It's also written well, is breezy reading, and makes you think."
—**Dr. Joe Vitale**, author, *Life's Missing Instruction Manual*

*Craig Franklin generously funded
the Second Printing of this book.*

# Secrets of
# LIBERTARIAN
# PERSUASION

## Michael Cloud

THE ADVOCATES FOR SELF-GOVERNMENT

"If You Always Do" ©1978 by Michael Cloud.
"Five Iron Laws of Government" ©1995 by Michael Cloud.
Weight Watchers is a registered trademark of Weight Watchers International, Inc.
Wile E. Coyote and Road Runner are trademarks of Warner Bros. Entertainment Inc., and
©2003 Warner Bros. Entertainment Inc.
Scripture quotations taken from the *New American Standard Bible®*, Copyright ©1960,
1962, 1963, 1968, 1971, 1972, 1973, 1975, 1977, 1995 by The Lockman Foundation.
Used by permission. (www.Lockman.org)
"Small government is beautiful" is a registered service mark of Carla Howell.
"Personal responsibility sets us free" is a registered service mark of Michael Cloud.

Most of the essays in this book originally appeared in slightly different form in the
*Liberator Online* or the *Libertarian Communicator,* published by the Advocates for
Self-Government.

First printing, May 2004
Second printing, January 2007

Cloud, Michael
*Secrets of Libertarian Persuasion*
By Michael Cloud
ISBN 0-9754326-1-3
1. Politics        2. Political persuasion        3. Libertarianism
4. Communications techniques
I. Title        II. Cloud, Michael

Manufactured in the United States of America
Typography and Cover Design by Bill Winter

*Dedicated to*

*Carla Howell*
*Extraordinary individual*
*Bold and brilliant libertarian leader*

# TABLE OF CONTENTS

## INSIGHTS & OUTLOOKS

# INTRODUCTION

Most books take too long to read.

Not this one.

This is a fast-paced book. With brief and readable chapters. You can read a chapter in minutes. You can read the whole book in a couple of hours.

You can start using the ideas and techniques today.

I hope you do.

Because you'll see the difference they make in libertarian conversations with your family, friends, and co-workers.

When you apply *Secrets of Libertarian Persuasion* methods to your libertarian knowledge, you'll start seeing changes in the way that others respond to you.

You'll begin changing other peoples' minds about libertarianism. Don't be surprised when you convince others to become libertarians.

You can begin today. With your next political conversation.

Other libertarians are reading *Secrets of Libertarian Persuasion.* They can begin today. With their next political conversation.

Together, we can change the world. We can advance the cause of individual liberty, personal responsibility, and small government.

Help make freedom possible. Learn and use the *Secrets of Libertarian Persuasion.*

Michael Cloud
Wayland, Massachusetts

# SECTION I

# STORIES

# Big Government As Wile E. Coyote

Ever watch Road Runner cartoons?

They explain the secret of government.

Road Runner is the free market. Road Runner moves fast and fends for himself.

He's self-reliant. An individualist. He doesn't interfere with others. He's free... as a bird.

Wile E. Coyote is Big Government. Wile E. Coyote wants to live off Road Runner.

Acme Products are Big Government programs.

Every episode, Wile E. Coyote unveils a brilliant new Acme product to get the Road Runner. Acme Products have great blueprints and schematics and seem foolproof.

Every episode, the brilliant new Acme product fails, smashes, crashes, explodes, careens, short-circuits, jams, and collapses. Wile E. Coyote is folded, spindled, mutilated, and crushed by the Acme product. Usually after the hapless coyote falls half a mile into a ravine.

Wile E. Coyote is hopelessly optimistic that the next Acme product will get Road Runner. In spite of the fact that every Acme product ever built has failed to get the bird.

Acme products makes huge profits selling these impossible schemes and unworkable products to a Coyote too dumb to notice that he never gets Road Runner — and always gets smashed by the new Acme product.

Wile E. Coyote is spending a fortune buying the next Acme product. A tax-funded fortune. For an Acme product and Coyote that will fail and fall on us.

Meanwhile, Road Runner eludes and evades, outruns and

outsmarts Wile E. Coyote and the new Acme product.

If the Coyote realized that Acme doesn't work, he might stop wasting our money... and maybe even stop bugging Road Runner.

The folks working at Acme could do something productive.

Road Runner could run farther and faster — and maybe even safely stop for birdseed now and then.

Road Runner will never be safe until he permanently shuts down Acme Products — and demands that Wile E. Coyote keeps his hands off roadrunners.

Next time someone proposes a new government program, next time someone calls for continuing to support and sustain a government program, remember Wile E. Coyote, label it "Acme Products" and answer...

"Beep-Beep."

# Welfare Pigeons

In the early 1970s, a group of scientists did an experiment called, "The Pigeon in a Welfare State." They took hungry pigeons and divided them into three groups: a control group, and two different test groups.

One test group learned to hop on a pedal to get grain. The other test group got the same grain, regardless of what they did.

The control group went hungry.

All three groups were put into cages where they had to learn to peck a lighted key to get grain. The group that had learned to hop on the pedal learned fastest. The control group learned much slower. And the pigeons who got fed no matter what were slowest.

Once they learned this lesson, they were put into new cages where they got fed when they refrained from pecking. Same results. The group that learned that their dinner depended on their own efforts did best. The control group was second. The welfare pigeons were last. Dead last.

People are not pigeons. People are far more intelligent and resourceful. But, like pigeons, we are dramatically influenced by our early learning experiences.

Think of a young boy whose parents are on government welfare. What lessons is he learning? That you don't have to work for a living. That diligent work, responsibility, and resourcefulness aren't necessary to get on in life.

He learns to be helpless. He learns that it pays off.

There are millions of boys and girls learning these lessons every day. Some day, they'll be parents. They will instill these lessons in their children. By example. And this legacy of learned helplessness will be passed down from generation to generation.

The government welfare system is undermining the American way of life. We must make certain that people are rewarded for their work. And that they must work for their rewards. Otherwise, we're the pigeons.

                         *      *      *

Aesop taught through fables.

Jesus taught through parables.

So did Uncle Remus. Abe Lincoln. The Buddha. Confucius.

Tales teach. Stories persuade.

What stories do you know that would illustrate the libertarian alternative?

What tales can you share that will set your hearers' hearts afire, with a love of individual liberty, personal responsibility, and small government?

As James Keller wrote, "Tell your tales; make them true. If they endure, so will you."

# Persuasion Lessons from the Gardener

"Michael, my father's a World War II veteran. How do I convince him that our libertarian non-interventionist policy is right?" asks one person.

"I know this guy who agrees with us on everything except immigration. I've given him books and tapes that make a strong case for open immigration. I've talked with him for hours. Nothing works. How do I change his mind?" asks another.

"I have a friend who won't even listen to me on the drug issue. How do I turn him around?" asks a third.

How do you break through people's resistance? How do you overcome some people's refusal to hear you out? How do you get through a person's stubbornness?

High-impact persuasion approaches can make you three to ten times as effective at changing people's minds.

But no matter how good you get, no matter how knowledgeable you become, no matter how completely you master libertarian persuasion, you will fail.

No one convinces every person on every issue every time. I don't. You won't. No one does.

Perhaps we can take persuasion lessons from the gardener.

Jesus tells a parable that shines light on this. In Matthew 13, Jesus says, "Behold, the sower went out to sow; and as he sowed, some seeds fell beside the road, and the birds came and ate them up.

"Others fell on the rocky places, where they did not have much soil; and immediately they sprang up, because they had no depth of soil. But when the sun had risen, they were scorched; and because they had no root, they withered away.

"Others fell among the thorns, and the thorns came up and choked them out.

"And others fell on the good soil and yielded a crop, some a hundredfold, some sixty, and some thirty."

Barren ground and a hostile climate can kill the strongest seeds.

Fertile soil and a friendly climate can nurture even weak seeds.

Between barren soil with a hostile climate and fertile soil with a friendly climate is the domain of the master gardener.

Here are the persuasion lessons from the master gardener.

1. Use quality seed. Use the best libertarian ideas and examples and evidence. From Ayn Rand, Frederic Bastiat, Henry Hazlitt, Murray Rothbard, Charles Murray, and Harry Browne.

2. Seek out fertile soil and a friendly climate. Even if you make mistakes, they will nurture the growth of libertarianism.

3. Properly prepare the soil before planting. We must plow and fertilize and water the soil, so it's most receptive to the seeds.

4. Timing makes a difference. If we plant an idea too early, or when a person is argumentative or angry, or when he's not interested... we increase the odds that the seed will shrivel and die. And that the soil will remain inhospitable to libertarian ideas.

5. The strongest plants develop their own roots. Too much fertilizer or too much water weakens the plants. Ideas and plants must struggle a little to become strong.

6. No matter how good the gardener, nor how strong the seed, some plants will die.

We can become better gardeners. We can gather better tools and seed.

Even master gardeners reap failures. Some seeds fail. Some plants die.

But master gardeners grow prize-winners year after year. Master gardeners grow better and bigger gardens every season.

And these gardens of liberty can feed the world.

Become a master gardener.

# Chinese Bamboo...
# A Story Retold

Chinese farmers raise an interesting variety of bamboo. One day they plant and fertilize the bamboo. They water it properly.

They water it all spring and summer. No bamboo breaks through the soil. The next year, they water their fields. No bamboo comes up. The next year and the next year, they water it still.

Finally, the fifth year, bamboo shoots break through the topsoil. In a period of six weeks, the Chinese bamboo grows 90 feet tall.

*Ninety feet of growth in only six weeks!*

Why? How?

For five years, the Chinese bamboo was developing a root structure capable of supporting and sustaining a 90-foot plant.

For five years, the Chinese bamboo was securing its foundations.

For five years, the Chinese bamboo was preparing to break through... and rise.

Suppose the farmers had deserted the fields after one year because no bamboo had broken through.

Suppose the farmers had quit after two years because they believed that "the crop was a failure."

Suppose they walked away after three years or four years because their "more practical" neighbors were able to grow weeds year after year with little effort.

Chinese bamboo takes care and cultivation to raise.

It takes a long view to begin. And faith and endurance to see it through.

The libertarian movement may be like Chinese bamboo.
Some sprouts are just beginning to see sunlight.
Others may break though soon.
We must water and nurture them.
We must plant more and more and more libertarian seeds...
so that when the massive, swift growth happens... it happens
*everywhere* in America.

# The Better Mousetrap Myth

*"If a man can write a better book, preach a better sermon, or make a better mousetrap than his neighbor, though he build his house in the woods, the world will make a beaten path to his door."* — Attributed to Ralph Waldo Emerson

Many people believe that better products and better ideas will naturally triumph.

Others act as if they believe that the marketplace will reward those who provide the best goods and services.

History is filled with those who built better mousetraps — and saw weeds grow through untaken paths to their doors. Many died unknown, only to be discovered a lifetime later.

George Ohm, the electrical researcher, was ignored because he was "only a Jesuit math teacher."

The pioneer geneticist Gregor Mendel went unnoticed because he was a rural priest.

Ignaz Philipp Semmelweis, the father of medical sterilization, was spurned. So were his impressive empirical results.

A history of science chronicles hundreds of neglected paths to better mousetraps.

The arts fared no better. Vincent Van Gogh sold two paintings during his lifetime. Franz Kafka was unknown. William Shakespeare was considered a hack who wrote for the rabble.

Inventions? The Xerox process was invented during the 1930s. It took 25 years to get it to market. Edwin Land invented "instant developing" and tried to sell the process to Kodak. They said there was no market for it. Polaroid was his answer.

A man in Ohio invented the vacuum cleaner. He went broke.

He finally asked a man named William H. Hoover to produce
and sell it. Hoover nearly went belly-up trying to convince
stores to sell vacuum cleaners.

Why? Stores claimed that there was no market for vacuum
cleaners.

Brooms were cheap and reliable.

In desperation, Hoover set up a door-to-door sales force. He
created a market for vacuum cleaners.

In science and art and inventions, creative individuals built
better mousetraps. But the world failed to beat a path to their
doors.

Why?

"Nothing happens until someone sells something," said Red
Motley.

"Production minus sales equals scrap," added a sales trainer.

Goods and products must be advertised. Must be marketed.
Must be sold.

So, too, with ideas and ideals.

Individual liberty, personal responsibility, and small
government must be advertised and marketed and sold.

We cannot simply create and refine our libertarian philosophy
— and wait for the world to beat a path to our door.

What is the most powerful advertising?

Word-of-mouth.

Are you word-of-mouth advertising our better libertarian
mousetrap?

Are your conversations selling other people on the direct,
huge, immediate benefits of our libertarian proposals?

Are you word-of-mouth marketing libertarianism to people
who haven't heard our ideas?

Are you "asking for the order"? Are you asking people to
"buy" by supporting the libertarian organizations you support?
Are you asking them to take your favorite organization out for
a "test drive" and then get happily involved?

You can't sell what you haven't bought.

Are you checking out tools, books, tapes, and other
libertarian products from libertarian organizations? Are you
spending money with and contributing to the libertarian organizations you believe in?

Are you distributing the World's Smallest Political Quiz to

waitresses in restaurants, to students, to your fellow church members, to your family, and to others?

Are you turbo-charging your libertarian persuasion skills by listening to and learning from tapes like "The Essence of Political Persuasion"?

The better mousetrap must be advertised. The better mousetrap must be marketed. The better mousetrap must be sold.

Mostly by word-of-mouth advertising. Word-of-mouth marketing.

Word-of-mouth selling.

Yours. And mine.

# A Lesson from Rosa Parks

Thirty years ago, I got the chance to hear a speech by Rosa Parks. The African-American woman who refused to go to the back of the bus. The woman who refused to allow Jim Crow segregation laws to make her a second-class citizen. The woman who helped launch the Montgomery bus boycott — and the modern civil rights movement. Rosa Parks.

As I sat in the audience, I wondered, "What was it like for Rosa Parks and Ralph Abernathy and Martin Luther King when they began their quest? Were they scared? Were they intimidated by the magnitude of the task? Did they get discouraged? Did they ever consider giving up?"

Because I faced the same questions — as a libertarian.

Rosa Parks gave an evocative and tender speech. We showered her with much-deserved applause.

For almost an hour, the audience asked her questions — and she answered.

Finally, the event ended, most of the audience left, and perhaps 20 of us hung around until she had to leave.

She said, "Thank you for your kindness. But I have to go."

That's when I got my chance to ask Rosa Parks my question.

"Ms. Parks?" I asked. "When you refused to go to the back of that bus... when you stepped off that bus... when you began the Montgomery bus boycott... *How* did you know that you'd win?"

She busted out laughing.

"Child, don't you know anything?" said Rosa Parks. "When you begin, you can't know. You act from faith in your cause. You just put one foot in front of the other... and march into history."

Thank you, Rosa Parks.

That was a lesson for this libertarian. A lesson for all of us.

Like Rosa Parks, libertarians "can just put one foot in front of the other... and march into history."

# Ben Franklin's Road
# to Excellence

"Michael, I've listened to your 'Essence of Political Persuasion' tapes several times. I read your 'Persuasion Power Points' column in the *Liberator Online*. I've listened to 'The Freedom Store,' and 'Personal Responsibility Is the Price of Liberty.' I've read Harry Browne. But when I get in a conversation about libertarian ideas, I get flustered. I get confused. I don't know which ideas and persuasion techniques to use. How do I get better at persuading people? I really care about liberty. How do I improve my persuasive skills?" asked Jan T.

"I understand how you feel," I said. "I felt the same way as I learned these things. I got really confused and frustrated. Then I got lucky. I read Ben Franklin's autobiography... and learned Ben Franklin's Road to Excellence. Would you like to hear how he solved the problem?"

"Absolutely," Jan replied.

"Ben Franklin thought of himself as a person of ordinary ability. But he believed that he could excel... if only he could find a method to acquire the essentials of successful living.

"He made a list of 13 virtues that he wanted to turn into personal habits. Then he hit upon an elegant and simple method for mastering them.

"Franklin decided to concentrate on one of the 13 habits each week. The first week he worked on Temperance: 'Eat not to dullness, drink not to elevation.'

"For seven days, he worked on improving his Temperance. During this week, he left the other 12 virtues to chance.

"The next week he worked on the second virtue, this time leaving Temperance and the other 11 virtues to chance.

"He did this for 13 weeks, then he repeated it. Then he repeated it again. At the end of a year, he had gone through his virtues four times. He found himself more successful and effective than he had ever been before. All because he focused his efforts.

"Jan, when we learn new ideas and techniques for communicating, most of us make one of two mistakes:

"We make no special effort to master the skill or technique. We've read the material, we've listed to the tapes, and we expect somehow the behavior will emerge in our conversations. This is the 'Leave it to Chance' non-method. It almost always fails.

"We get excited by all the great new ideas, information, and techniques. We resolve to start using *everything!* We're going to give it our all. This is the 'Immediate, Total Perfection' method. This is the fast-track to failure, confusion, and feelings of inadequacy.

"Ben Franklin's approach enables us to master several techniques by concentrating on one at a time.

"May I make a suggestion, Jan? Take six techniques from my 'Persuasion Power Points' columns in the *Liberator Online* and use the Ben Franklin method on them.

"Try these six persuasion techniques:
- The Magic 'If'
- The Reverse
- The Neglected Art of Listening
- Six-Step Recipe for Cooking Big Government
- Are You Tied in Nots?
- The Wrong End of the Stick

"Take six 3x5 index cards, and print the name of each technique at the top of the card. Make columns for each day of the week from Sunday through Saturday.

"Start your first week's practice with The Magic 'If.' At the beginning of each day, re-read the article from beginning to end. This will only take a few minutes.

"Each day, carry the card with you. Look for opportunities to use The Magic 'If' in political and personal conversations. Each time you use the technique, make a mark on that day's column. This way you can see how many times you used the technique each day.

"Why make a mark for each time you use the technique? Whatever gets measured, gets done. Whatever gets measured frequently, gets done frequently. And frequent measurement leads to improvements in the quantity and quality of the behavior you're measuring.

"So the first week, you'll get a lot better at using The Magic 'If.'

"You'll become more sensitive to opportunities for using the technique. You'll become more skilled and confident in very short order.

"The next week you'll work on The Reverse. And so on, until you go through all six techniques. I suggest you go through the set at least three full times. Notice how much more often you use each technique. And how much more comfortable, confident, and capable you are with each one.

"Jan, this is how I practiced the Art of Libertarian Persuasion. This is how the best athletes, musicians, and other artists practice their performances. This is Ben Franklin's Road to Excellence."

# George Bernard Shaw's Tailor

"My tailor is the only man who really understands me," said George Bernard Shaw. "He takes my measure anew each time we meet."

Most of us aren't as wise as George Bernard Shaw's tailor.

We see people we haven't seen for years, and we tell them, "You haven't changed a bit!"

Or, "You're the same as you always were."

Are they really the same?

Or are we forgetting to take their measure anew?

Social psychology has a name for this: the High School Reunion Phenomenon.

At our tenth year reunion, or twentieth year reunion, we see people we haven't seen since high school.

We talk about old times. We relive glory days. We reminisce.

Then we go home and say, "I've changed a lot, but they're the same as they ever were."

Are they?

When we go to high school reunions, we're scanning for similarities. Our memories are primed to find people who look just like, sound just like, and act just like the kids we went to high school with. Only older. And wrinkly-er.

We're looking for similarities. So that's what we find.

We know that we've changed.

Or have we?

If we rode home with some of the people that we'd just seen for the first time in 10 or 20 years, we'd hear them saying, "Boy they haven't changed a bit... but I have."

We didn't take their measure anew. And they didn't take ours.

George Bernard Shaw's tailor was right. People do change. And unless we look for change, we'll miss it.

This is crucial to persuasion.

People change their values. People change themselves. And events change people.

Changed values and changed lives mean new opportunities for communicating libertarianism.

Changed values and changed lives mean new wants and needs. New situations. New concerns and interests. New conversational openings.

If we assume that the person we were talking with "hasn't changed a bit," we might miss out on the fact that they just got audited by the IRS. Do you think that might make them more receptive to libertarian tax cut and tax repeal proposals?

If we forget to take the person's measure anew, we might never know that one of their close friends or family members has been sentenced to 10 years in federal prison for a marijuana offense. They might be open to the idea of ending Drug Prohibition.

If we overlook the fact that people are always changing, we might not hear about a friend being stalked or threatened. We might never know that they are ripe for a discussion of gun ownership and the right to protect themselves and their families.

If we neglect to look for how the person has changed, we might not learn that they are expecting a baby... and might be eager to hear about homeschooling. Or separating school and state.

What can George Bernard Shaw's tailor teach us?

Actively look for what's different when you meet people again. Actively ask what's different.

Seek and scan for changes in their lives. Explore the changes. Ask them to talk about the changes since you last got together.

What's new in their lives? New activities. New people. New events. New feelings and values. Invite people to talk about the novel and new.

Comment on and, where appropriate, compliment them for positive changes. Drop them notes mentioning how healthy and good they look since they've lost the weight. Or since they got their promotion. Send them notes and emails giving them warm feedback on the changes.

Change is opportunity. A new chance to build libertarian bridges to other people's lives.

And we might miss this opportunity.

Unless we emulate George Bernard Shaw's tailor.

# Mark Twain's Cat

Mark Twain had a cat.

One day, his cat jumped on a hot stove. He jumped right back down.

That cat never jumped on a hot stove again.

Of course, he never jumped on a cold stove either.

Sometimes, we make the same mistakes that Mark Twain's cat made.

Most of our political discussions are driven by current events. When something's in the news, we analyze and debate the issue. The subject is hot.

The Columbine High School shooting. Teenagers are tragically killed. The issue of firearms is hot. So we discuss guns. The subject's red hot. We jump on that stove, and we get burned.

There's a news story about kids dying from impure street drugs. The subject is hot. So we discuss drug issues.

The subject's red hot. We jump on that stove, and we get burned.

Public school test scores and SAT's plummet. You have friends with kids in public schools. Your friends are calling for school bonds, charter schools, performance testing, vouchers... because *something* must be done now!

The subject's sizzling and simmering. We jump on that stove, and we get burned again.

Many of us make the same mistake as Mark Twain's cat.

We're afraid of the stove. But the real problem is the heat.

Breaking news of an emergency or tragedy. When an event is *the* news event of the hour or day or week, few people are capable of calm, thoughtful, and wise analysis.

When a disaster is unfolding, when a calamity is developing and getting worse, emotions flare and people demand decisive action.

When passions are inflamed, when people are afraid, they panic. They overreact. They are neither willing nor able to give their best thought to the matter.

This is the worst time to discuss abstract philosophy, principles of politics, or the blessings of liberty.

The worst time to try to persuade. The stove's too hot. Too hot for us. Too hot for them. We need a cooling-off period.

Because the problem is the temperature, not the stove.

If we want understanding, not anger, we must let the stove cool. Wait a few weeks after the emergency or tragedy has ended. Then examine the event in the light of liberty.

How did government policies contribute to the tragedy? How did government laws and regulations prevent us from foreseeing and averting the tragedy? How did government programs and mandates make the problem worse?

If these policies and laws and programs and mandates did *not* exist, how and why would things have turned out dramatically better?

For example, in *Losing Ground* by Charles Murray, we were shown the empirical chapter and verse of how government social policies injured the very people they were trying to help.

Professor Murray documented how and where these government programs from 1950 to 1980 made things dramatically worse.

He learned the lesson that Mark Twain's cat did not. Charles Murray waited until the stove had cooled. To powerful effect.

We can discuss issues when they're cold or warm. But not when they're red hot.

Not until cool heads can prevail.

So when the news is blaring and scaring us, when an emergency is erupting or unfolding, we must be patient. This is *not* the time to present libertarian analyses or solutions.

Bide your time. Let the stove cool. Wait a few weeks.

Then the emergency or tragedy can be touched upon without fear. It can be examined more calmly and comfortably.

Because we must get beyond the heat to the light.

# Thomas Edison's Lesson

Thomas Edison is reputed to have tried 10,000 experiments before he found a filament for the light bulb.

A shining example of persistence?

"If at first you don't succeed, try, try again." Is that the lesson of Thomas Edison?

No.

Thomas Edison was asked how it felt to have failed 10,000 times.

"I didn't fail," said the inventor. "I found 10,000 ways *not* to make a light bulb."

Edison did not "try, try again."

Or, more accurately, he didn't try the same thing again and again and again.

He tried 10,000 *different* ways to make a light bulb.

But that's not the lesson we're taught.

Here's what we're taught:

If something doesn't work, do it again.

If something doesn't work, do it repeatedly.

If something doesn't work, do it harder.

If something doesn't work, do it longer.

If yelling doesn't work, yell again. Yell repeatedly. Yell harder. Yell longer. Yell louder.

It's not working, so do it again.

This approach misses Thomas Edison's lesson.

Thomas Edison's experimental approach tells us:

If what you're doing doesn't work, stop doing it.

If what you're doing doesn't work, do something else.

If that something else doesn't work, do a different something else.

Keep doing different things until you find what does work. Then do what works.

There's your filament. There's your light bulb.

That's Thomas Edison's lesson.

We all make this mistake. We get stuck.

We repeat what doesn't work.

Again and again and again.

As Edna St. Vincent Millay said, "It is not true that life is one damn thing after another — it's one damn thing over and over." So is repeating what does not work.

Perhaps you've discussed separating school and state with friends.

Maybe they can't even imagine an alternative to government-run public schools.

"What if some parents didn't send their kids to school?" "What about poor children? Who would pay for their education?" "How would we make sure we have qualified teachers?" "What if the religious right tried to brainwash children into believing that the Bible is literally true?" "What if the ultra-liberals encourage children to experiment with drugs or sex?"

So you discuss and debate the issue with your friends. They're not buying. So you give them more evidence and arguments. You discuss and debate the issue with your friends again. And again. Longer. Harder. Louder.

What you're doing doesn't work. And yet you repeat it again and again.

It's an easy trap to fall into.

We've all been there.

And we're likely to find ourselves there again. And again and again.

Unless we learn Thomas Edison's lesson.

For example, maybe your friends are not open to our approach on education. But perhaps they're open to our position on the War on Drugs. Or gun freedom. Or small government.

If education discussions don't work, discuss something else.

If your approach to education doesn't work, approach education differently.

Perhaps from the direction of parental authority. Or that of diversity. Or free enterprise virtues and values.

If what you're doing doesn't work, do something else.

If what you're talking about doesn't work, talk about something else.

If how you're talking about it doesn't work, talk about it in a different way.

If who you're talking to isn't working out, talk to someone else.

Some people succeed by reinventing the wheel. Most people fail by reinventing the flat tire.

Some people fail repeatedly when they fail to change the flat tire. Or try to sell flat tires to friends.

If your persuasion approach doesn't work, stop doing it.

If your persuasion approach doesn't work, try something different.

If your second persuasion approach doesn't work, try a third approach.

Keep trying different approaches until you find one that works.

Then do what works.

There's your filament. There's your light bulb.

That's Thomas Edison's lesson for those who want to persuade.

# No Paine, No Gain

"Where freedom is, there is my home," said Benjamin Franklin.

"Where freedom is *not*, there is mine," responded Thomas Paine.

These represent two different approaches for libertarians. Two very different motives.

Benjamin Franklin and his spiritual children want to live *in* freedom. Thomas Paine and his spiritual children want to live *for* freedom. Franklin's followers want to embrace and enjoy the blessings of liberty. Paine's admirers seek to bestow the blessings of liberty on others.

Every free society needs its Benjamin Franklin. And its Thomas Paine.

Today's libertarians choose the path of Paine or the path of Franklin.

Franklin's followers want to talk with other libertarians. Be with other libertarians. Read libertarian books and magazines. Immerse themselves in the libertarian world.

This gives them a sense of identity and community. It lets them speak a common language. And it gives them a sense that all is right in their world.

The Franklin approach attracts new libertarians. It gives them a chance to devour and digest libertarian philosophy. It lets them familiarize themselves with the principles and applications of liberty.

This is a good place to start. And a good place to return home to from time to time.

But Franklin's world is not enough.

It survives only at the pleasure of Big Government. Only by permission. Only by the regulations not enforced and the laws not passed.

Until America is fully free, Franklin's world is a world of fiction and fantasy.

It is not enough. Not nearly enough.

No Paine, no gain.

Thomas Paine's path leads us to people who could be libertarians. People who should be libertarians. People who would be libertarians... if we would reach out.

Thomas Paine's path calls for us to stretch and risk and grow.

Paine's libertarian path means inviting and evangelizing.

It demands we share the good news.

Celebrate the values and virtues of liberty with those who have never seen nor heard them.

It demands we shower libertarian ideas and insights and solutions on new and fertile fields.

It inspires us to offer libertarian videos and CDs and books to people we've just met.

- Why not get a video copy of *John Stossel Goes To Washington*? It's only $29.95. Invite five or six *non*-libertarian friends over for a get-together. Get out the popcorn or tortilla chips. Fire up the VCR. And let John Stossel do Paine's work for you. Then ask your guests, "What did you like best about the video? What did you find most interesting? Where did you agree most with John Stossel?" (If you do this right, you should grin like the Cheshire cat.)

- Why not get a copy of my "Personal Responsibility is the Price of Liberty" CD set from the Advocates? Why not loan it to a *non*-libertarian friend with the following request: "I just listened to this really interesting talk about personal responsibility. If I loaned it to you, would you be willing to listen to it tomorrow while you drive to work?" (If they've been resistant to individual liberty... turn the coin over and let me introduce them to personal responsibility.)

- Why not buy a gift copy of *The Great Libertarian*

*Offer* by Harry Browne for a *non*-libertarian friend? Pick one chapter you think will really resonate with your friend. Ask them to read that chapter first, then ask them to tell you what they liked best about that section. After you've talked with them about it, ask them to read the whole book, cover-to-cover. (Let Harry Browne sell freedom to your friend.)

If we want to have more freedom to share, we must share the freedom we have.

"Where freedom is not, there is my home," said Thomas Paine.

Open your spiritual home to strangers. Open your heart to new faces. Speak with those you've never spoken with before.

The only way to reach the world of Benjamin Franklin is the path of Thomas Paine.

Reach out and grow the libertarian movement.

Bring in new members.

No Paine, no gain.

# Richard Feynman's Roadmap

I recently received an email message from a new libertarian. He had just heard about a new persuasive technique. "What do you think of this technique?" he asked me. "Do you think it would work? What's your opinion?" While this reader's intentions were good, this is the *wrong* question.

Why?

A persuasive technique is a tool. An instrument to achieve a specific outcome.

If I went to a hardware store and asked the owner, "What do you think of this hammer?" he'd tell me what it was made of and why it was made that way. He'd tell me what do-it-yourself handymen told him about the hammer.

But how would I find out whether the hammer was the tool I really needed?

I would buy it and try it.

I would experiment with it. Use it. See how well it served my purposes.

Richard Feynman probably put it best, "Scientists are explorers. Philosophers are tourists."

In *Surely You're Joking, Mr. Feynman,* the Nobel Prize-winning physicist gives anecdotes and examples that illustrate one crucial fact about science: It tests its hypotheses against reality. As Feynman noted, "Nature will not be fooled."

Feynman would tell us to take a persuasive technique... and test it. Again and again. To measure the results. Again and again.

Philosopher libertarians ask, "What do you think about this approach? In your opinion, is this useful? What are your reasons?"

Scientist libertarians ask, "What have you tried? How many people did you try it on? Did it work or not? How well? When, where and how did you test this technique?"

"Nature will not be fooled."

Don't debate a technique, test it.

Don't argue about a persuasive tool, try it.

Count. Measure. Record. Compare.

Persuasive technology is an empirical science. Not a deductive endeavor.

How do I know? Thirty years ago, I began reading Ayn Rand, Austrian economists, and others whose approach is primarily deductive. They would begin with axioms or First Principles. Then they would derive their theories using self-evident truths and the laws of logic.

I, too, would start with axioms and the laws of logic. I would take my new "certainties" out into the world "of shoes, and ships, and sealing wax, of cabbages and kings..." and they would fail. Dismally. Totally.

"Nature will not be fooled."

I discovered the hard way what Ayn Rand explained in "Who Is the Final Authority In Ethics?" (*The Objectivist Newsletter*, Vol. 4, No. 2, February 1965).

Reality has the final word. Reality has the first word. And every word in between.

Especially with persuasive techniques. Or approaches. Or phrases. Or behavioral recipes.

I learned to try out every persuasive tool I offer. To treat every tool as a hypothesis. And to use the scientific method to test it.

Here are a few ways you can test different approaches, without becoming a crash-test dummy:

1. **Call a talk radio show.** Try the persuasive script on the listening audience. Ask them to call in to the talk show host with their reaction. Does it produce the results you want? Does it reach a higher percentage of people than other approaches you've tried? Now call another talk radio show. And another. Test it a dozen times. Record the results. Good, bad, and ugly.

2. **Go to a bookstore.** Find a book browser. Tell the

person, "I just heard an interesting idea. This guy told me... (fill in the persuasive idea). What do you think of it?" Listen to their response. And watch their body language. Thank them for their thoughts. Now go find another book shopper. Do it again, with the same idea and the same phrasing. Try it on 12 people. Record your results. (And buy a good book while you're there!)

In less than 90 minutes, you'll have more first-hand experimental information about that persuasion technique than you could get from a month of thought and Internet research.

This real-world field test will make you more knowledgeable. More confident. More competent.

(A personal confession: I personally field-test my techniques in three bookstores in Massachusetts. So many experimental subjects, so little time...)

3. **Give a speech using the persuasive approach that you want to test.** Toastmasters. Churches. Service clubs. High school classes. Special interest organizations. Political groups. Give the same speech to three or four different groups. Their feedback will tell you whether it works or not. Whether it reaches their hearts and minds or not. Whether it changes their point of view or not.

You'll get good empirical data. *Plus* you'll get practice in delivering libertarian speeches.

*          *          *

Discard the techniques that don't work.

Use the techniques that do work. Use them again and again. Make them part of your persuasive toolbox.

Persuasive techniques must be tested. Experimented with. Tried. Used.

Results reveal which persuasive techniques belong in your libertarian toolbox. And which do not.

"Nature will not be fooled."

# The Black Door... Retold

Many years ago, in desert lands far away, there was a war. Fighting was fierce. Many were killed with sword and knife and gun.

As with all wars, there were leaders and generals and officers and common soldiers.

And spies.

Spies to sneak into enemy territory, gather vital information, sneak out, and give the information to their commanders.

Captured soldiers were treated honorably. Humanely.

But spies? Those who sneak and deceive? Those who deal in treachery?

Death to spies. Hanging. The firing squad. Or worse.

In this desert war, one fort commander came up with a terrifying punishment for spies.

When captured and convicted, the spy was brought before this fort commander and given a choice: execution by firing squad or... The Black Door.

The convicted spy was sent back to his cell for the night. To reason and worry and decide.

Every spy had heard the whisperings and rumors and stories about The Black Door. "What's behind that cursed door?" cried the prisoner. "Slow, painful torture? A snake pit? Staked down to an ant hill? What unspeakable evils await me behind The Black Door?"

At daybreak, the spy was brought before the fort commander. "Which shall it be: the firing squad... or The Black Door?"

Terror in his eyes, the spy said, "The firing squad."

Moments later, shots rang out. The spy was dead.

A young officer, just assigned to the fort, was overcome with curiosity.

"Commander," he said, "I am new here. Please tell me. What lies behind The Black Door?"

"Freedom," responded the commander. "But few have the courage to choose it."

\*      \*      \*

And so it is.

As long as freedom is a Black Door, few will have the courage to step through it.

As long as freedom is a dark unknown, an ominous risk... few will embrace it.

As long as freedom is the stuff of fear and foreboding, few will have the courage to choose it.

Libertarians must open The Black Door. We must shine the light of wisdom and knowledge on what lies behind it.

We must read and write, listen and speak, learn and teach others the lessons of liberty.

We must show people the glorious sunlit liberty that awaits us on the other side of The Black Door.

# The Baruch Question

Bernard Baruch was one of the most successful stock investors of all time.

He foresaw the stock market crash of 1929 — and sold his stocks near peak value.

He continued to make huge profits during the Great Depression.

In today's dollars, Baruch earned billions. He died rich.

What was his secret?

Bernard Baruch used a simple technique to evaluate the stocks in his portfolio.

Every morning, he'd see what his stocks were selling for.

Then he'd ask himself, "Would I buy this stock today?"

If the answer was "Yes," he'd hold onto the stock, and perhaps buy more. If the answer was "No," he'd sell it.

He did *not* ask, "What did I originally pay for this stock?" Nor, "How long have I held it?"

Nor, "How can I justify taking a loss?"

He did *not* fall into what Harry Browne calls "The Previous Investment Trap."

He didn't let his past dictate his future.

Baruch asked, "If I didn't own this stock, would it be a good investment today? Would I buy it for the first time now?"

The Baruch Question is a powerful decision-making tool.

Apply it to the company you work for. If you had never worked for them, would you apply for a job with them today?

Apply it to your romantic partner. Would you marry her today? More importantly, would she marry you today?

If the answer is "Yes," great. But what if the answer is "No"?

Do you quit your job or pack your bags and move out?
In some cases, yes.

But in many other situations, the Baruch Question can help you zero in on what's missing or wrong. This information may lead you to new possibilities, new choices, and a better life. Perhaps a few months later, you'll ask the Baruch Question again — and discover your answer is "Yes."

Let's address the Baruch Question to your involvement in the libertarian movement.

If you had never invested any time and effort in the libertarian movement...

If you had never donated any money to a libertarian organization...

If you were looking at the libertarian movement for the first time...

Would *you* get involved, would you join... *today?*

Your response may touch upon several related questions:

1. How important is freedom to you?
2. What price are you willing to pay — in time, effort, and money — for the *chance* of freedom? Lots of people would like to be free — if it cost them nothing. TANSTAAFL: There Ain't No Such Thing As A Free Lunch. What price are you ready and willing to pay for liberty?
3. Is the libertarian movement an effective environment for advancing liberty? Which part of it is the best place for you to be involved?
4. Is the libertarian movement growing or shrinking? Is it becoming more effective or less effective?

Metaphors may help you answer the Baruch Question.

If the libertarian movement were a stock, and you had to chart its market value from 1993 through today — the last 10 years — what would the graph look like?

If you were an investor, and the libertarian movement were a stock, would it be a good value today?

Is the market over-valuing or under-valuing the libertarian movement? Would you buy it today?

If the libertarian movement were a business, and it tried to hire you, would you take the job?

If you answer "No," what are you going to do about it? Leave the libertarian movement?

Change it?

What needs to be changed to turn your answer into a "Yes"?

What needs to be added? Removed? Modified?

Specifically, what would it take to turn the libertarian movement into a great movement to join today?

Take the initiative. Embrace personal responsibility.

Start making these changes in yourself and your personal libertarian circles.

Alone, if necessary. With others, when possible.

Begin now.

Your choices and actions will help determine whether the libertarian movement shrinks or expands, weakens or strengthens, falls or rises.

Your decisions and behavior may influence future libertarians' responses to the Baruch Question. Next year. And into the future.

# Henry Hazlitt's Lesson

In *Economics in One Lesson* Henry Hazlitt taught us that, "The art of economics consists in looking not merely at the immediate but at the longer effects of any government act or policy; it consists in tracing the consequences of that government policy not merely for one group, but for all groups." He warned us against the "fallacy of overlooking secondary consequences" of a government program or policy.

Henry Hazlitt noted that good economists connect government action to its market consequences. Not just the consequences to special interests or targeted beneficiaries, but economic consequences to *all* groups. Direct and indirect. Immediate and secondary.

Good economists track consequences — and consequences of consequences.

Henry Hazlitt's lesson is brilliantly simple economic wisdom. And it's a vital persuasion power point for libertarians.

When examining a Big Government program or policy, we must follow its rippling waves of consequences. We must look beyond the "intended consequences" and "target" of the Big Government program or policy.

What are the consequences to un-targeted groups? Direct and indirect? Immediate and secondary? What are the consequences of the consequences?

What is the impact of the Big Government program on this group or that? Does the cost of the program make their lives better or worse? Do the consequences and consequences of the consequences make their lives better or worse? Exactly how?

What kind of behaviors does the Big Government program

reward or penalize, encourage or discourage?

How will people in each group respond to these costs and consequences? Will their behavior stay the same — or change? And what will be the consequences of that?

Ticking off seven bad consequences of Drug Prohibition can shake people awake.

Trotting out six dangerous results of anti-gun laws can make people stop, look, and listen.

Listing eight nasty outcomes of government-mandated single-payer medical care can be pure oxygen for a listener.

Counting off five harmful consequences of raising minimum wage laws can put many brains into the ranks of the employed.

To expand on Henry Hazlitt's lesson: Good libertarian communicators track consequences of Big Government's actions — and consequences of consequences.

But *after* we apply and illustrate this lesson, we must ask our listener one of my personal impact questions:

"How do you feel about that?"

Or: "Is that what you want?"

Or: "Is that acceptable to you?"

Then offer the libertarian alternative. The freedom solution. And the dramatically better consequences that liberty causes — and makes possible.

# The Myth of Mushrooms
# In the Night

Six months before the general election, an unknown libertarian files for public office. He holds a news conference in front of the federal building. His statement catalogs the damage caused by Big Government, declares the importance of individual freedom, and gives compelling reasons for electing him to office. Newspapers, radio, and television carry his message to the voters.

Day after day, for six months, this libertarian speaks out at civic events, public gatherings, colleges, and the like. He grants newspaper interviews, appears on radio and television talk shows, and goes before endorsement committees.

His message gets through. The voters come to their senses, realize their true interests, and catapult the libertarian into office.

This scenario is neat, simple, and wrong. It's the myth of mushrooms in the night.

A young boy goes to bed on a warm spring evening. The next morning, he awakens to a front yard covered with legions of mushrooms. Yesterday, the yard was uninterrupted green. Today, without any effort or time, mushrooms have sprung up. Without planning or cause. A touch of magic, a hint of the miraculous has entered his life.

It may be several years before the lad learns the natural causes of mushroom growth. Until then, he sees magic, not science. He believes in the Easter Bunny, Santa Claus, the Tooth Fairy, elves — and mushrooms that magically spring up in the night.

As the boy matures, he discards these childhood fantasies.

Or, rather, most of them. Some otherwise mature adults nourish and cherish a belief in the magical. They cling to the myth of mushrooms in the night.

Everyone has dreamed of becoming an overnight success. Wouldn't it be wonderful to wake up one morning and find you've inherited a million dollars? Or written a best-selling novel? Or become a rock and roll star?

Wouldn't it be wonderful to awaken one morning to discover that you're the first libertarian governor or senator or president?

These dreams of overnight accomplishment can be a pleasant diversion. They can fuel our efforts to make something of our lives.

But some people forget that "the overnight success" is a myth, and begin to treat it as a real possibility. They rationalize and cultivate it as "a long shot."

In the libertarian movement, a few individuals subscribe to the myth of mushrooms in the night.

Perhaps they were captivated by *Atlas Shrugged*. They may remember John Galt's three-hour radio speech — and the effect it had on the millions who heard it.

They may have been influenced by libertarian science fiction. Robert Heinlein. Eric Frank Russell. F. Paul Wilson. James P. Hogan. Or the Matador series by Steve Perry.

Some libertarians were "overnight converts." On the basis of a conversation or a book, these individuals joined the libertarian movement. These rare ones may assume that there are thousands more like them.

Individuals act on the basis of their beliefs and assumptions.

If a libertarian harbors a belief in overnight success, in the myth of mushrooms in the night... and if he decides to run for office, what will he do?

He'll predict massive public support and high vote totals. He'll beg and borrow as much money as he can get his hands on — to pay for brochures, fliers, and TV, radio, and newspaper advertisements. He'll harass libertarians to give as much time and money as he has.

He may even take out a second mortgage on his home to get another $25,000 or $50,000 for his campaign. Or spend his life savings. He may take a six-week unpaid leave of absence from his job to campaign full-time.

He'll answer every candidate questionnaire he can. Speak at every open public event he can. Seek as much "free media" as possible.

He will believe, truly believe that he can win this important office.

On election night, one thing will be clear: He "failed." He fell embarrassingly short of his predictions and promises. So he rationalizes. Explains. Justifies. Blames and excuses.

In his wake, we find the burnt-out passions of new activists and donors, the mutilated hopes of idealists, and the mortgaged futures of those who thought they were investing in libertarian victory.

The American Revolution of 1776 was sold out slowly. Not overnight. It won't be brought back with a quick fix.

Restoring liberty will take planning, effort, and time. A permanent freedom must begin in the hearts and minds of informed and committed libertarians.

We must recruit, educate, and activate new members. We must locate and enroll those who already agree with us. We must persuade and bring in others. We must enroll and involve these men and women in the libertarian movement.

Most of these new libertarians will be eager to learn the implications and applications of libertarianism. The impact and value of liberty.

Because of their zeal and libertarian education, these new libertarian activists will be ready and able and willing to recruit, educate, and activate more new libertarians.

It is not enough to join and learn and tell.

We must act to achieve liberty. And that requires bright, well-trained libertarian activists. We must equip them with the tools and training necessary to boldly advance the libertarian cause. We must teach them how to powerfully and persuasively present libertarianism. How to invite and involve volunteers.

How to organize ballot initiatives to dramatically roll back taxes. How to raise funds for these projects — and how to promote them.

How to organize and run a libertarian political campaign. How to be an overachieving libertarian candidate. And much, much more.

One well-trained libertarian activist can have a greater impact than a hundred Big Government mediocrities. As we recruit, educate, and activate, we are sowing the seeds of long-term libertarian success. Not the spores of mushrooms. Rather the seeds of oaks and redwoods. They take longer to mature. But their forests last for generations.

SECTION II

# TECHNIQUES

# The Weight Watchers Test

One governor announces a 20% spending cut. Another governor proclaims a multi-billion dollar spending reduction. A third governor says that his proposal will save taxpayers a whopping billion dollars.

Should we break out the champagne? Are things finally moving in the right direction for libertarians? Will these governments get smaller?

No.

Magicians perform many illusions with sleight-of-hand.

Big Government politicians do it with sleight-of-mouth.

The first governor is cutting 20% off the top of a $3 billion increase. The budget will go up $2.4 billion this year.

The second governor is taking $4 billion dollars off the top of a $9 billion spending increase. State government spending will go up $5 billion.

The third governor got a lower interest rate on his state's $30 billion debt. The lower payment "saves" $1 billion in interest, while freeing up $100 million a year to expand government "social services" and hire more government workers.

Big Government got bigger.

But all we hear from the Big Government politicians and the news media are stories of shrinking tax revenues, spending reductions, and program cutbacks.

How do they get away with this? How do they make it look like government is staying the same size — or getting smaller?

**Big Government Adjustments and Comparisons**
Here are a few things they do.

## 1. Adjust the government budget for inflation.

If last year's state budget was $20 billion, and inflation was 5%, and this year's budget is $22 billion, they can argue, that "adjusted for inflation, this year's spending has only gone up 4.5%."

This might seem reasonable and fair — except for one thing. They do *not* adjust taxpayers' income for inflation. If your family income was $40,000 last year, if you didn't get a pay raise this year, and if inflation is 5%, then you are $2,000 poorer this year.

Adjusted for inflation, taxpayers are losing 5% this year — while government is gaining 4.5%.

Tax producers get gouged — while tax consumers benefit.

Whether Big Government politicians or the news media call the government spending adjustment "constant dollars," "cost of living," "indexing," "static purchasing power," or something else....

Where is the same adjustment, same treatment, and same consideration for productive, hard-working taxpayers?

## 2. Compare the government spending to the economy.

"Our state government spending is X% of our state's Gross Domestic Product — in the bottom half of all state governments. We're committed to fiscal conservatism and limited government."

"During the last 10 years, our state's Gross Domestic Product increased 108%, and state government spending only rose 79%. Government is taking a smaller share of a growing economic pie."

What does this have to do with whether government is big or small? Whether government authority and power is growing or shrinking?

## 3. Compare this government budget to other government budgets.

"We're in the bottom half of all state governments in terms of state spending. We are committed to limiting government."

"We're in the bottom half of all state governments in terms of per capita spending."

"Last year, our state spending was the thirteenth highest out of 50 states. This year, we're down to twentieth — pretty close to average."

They can compare the whole budget or any part of it to

other state budgets. Does our tax burden lighten because that of others grows heavier? Are we better off because they are worse off?

### The Weight Watchers Test

Tired of Big Government sleight-of-mouth on government spending and growth? Want truth-in-labeling in politics? Full disclosure? You won't find it in the newspapers. But you will find it at Weight Watchers.

Weight Watchers is a wonderful organization that uses honesty, common sense and tried and true experience to help people lose weight and get healthier.

Suppose you weigh 300 pounds — and come to Weight Watchers to lose weight and get healthier. They'll give you great information and support — to help you slim down.

But they want you to be honest with yourself. What did you eat — today? What exercise did you do — today?

Then the Weight Watchers Test:

*Get on the scale.* How much do you weigh — today? 300 pounds?

For a week or two weeks or a month, you'll make your own decisions about eating and exercising. You'll probably log what you do. You'll come to meetings. You'll learn and share. Support and be supported.

Then the Weight Watchers Test:

*Get on the scale.* How much do you weigh — today?

Two hundred and ninety pounds? You're moving in the right direction. Making progress.

Three hundred and ten pounds? You're moving in the wrong direction. How can we help you turn this around?

Weight Watchers is honest.

They will *not* adjust the scale so you can lie to yourself and others. They will *not* justify your weight by telling you that on the moon you would weigh 50 pounds. They will *not* condone sleight-of-mouth weighing cons and comparisons:

"Well, my four closest friends started at 300 pounds like me, but now they weigh 330 pounds, while I only weigh 310 pounds. So... I'm really 20 pounds lighter."

"Because obesity is rapidly increasing in the United States, even though I gained 20 pounds, I'm much closer to the average weight than I was a year ago."

Weight Watchers wants you to be honest with yourself. *Get on the scale.* How much do you weigh — today? Are you heavier or lighter than last time? Is your weight going up or down?

Apply the Weight Watchers Test to government spending. Put government on the scale. How much did it spend this year?

How much did government spend last year?

Is government spending higher or lower than last year's spending? How much? Is this department's spending higher or lower than last year? How much?

How much higher or lower is government spending than it was 10 years ago? How much higher or lower is this department's spending than it was 10 years ago?

Is government bigger or smaller than it was last year? Is this department bigger or smaller than it was last year?

How much bigger or smaller is government than it was 10 years ago? How much bigger or smaller is this department than it was 10 years ago?

The Weight Watchers Test of government lets us know where we are, which direction we're moving...and how fast we're going.

The Weight Watchers Test of government frees us from sleight-of-mouth and political illusions.

It offers us the facts, the truth:

Are we moving toward bigger and bigger Big Government.... or getting closer and closer to individual liberty, personal responsibility, and small government?

# The Magic "If"

You're in the middle of a political discussion. You suggest a terrific libertarian solution to the problem of poverty or crime or a better world. You explain how and why our libertarian proposal would solve the problem quickly and cheaply — and leave us dramatically better off.

But the person you're talking to utters a killer phrase: "You can't do it because..."

"People will never support it because..."

Then he throws out reasons why your libertarian proposal will be untimely or impossible or unpopular.

If you're like most of us, you'll offer evidence and arguments to defend your libertarian solution, the other person will respond, and another no-win debate will take place.

Want to stop arguing — and start persuading?

The next time someone objects to your libertarian proposal or solution or remedy with "we can't because..." or "people will never support it because..."

Respond with:

- "You might be right." (Pause, then ask...) "But *if it were possible*... would you want it?"
- "You might be right. Most people might be against it today. But what if the majority changed its mind, what if we *did* implement it. Would it be a good thing?"
- "If it were up to you alone, would you want it?"

If the answer is "No," you can warmly finish up the conversation, and move on to someone who *does* want the blessings of liberty.

If the answer is "Yes," follow up with:

"Why would you want it?"

Or: "How would it make things better? What else would it accomplish?"

We spend hours overcoming objections and surmounting obstacles — only to discover that our challenger doesn't want what we're offering.

We spend too much time justifying the journey — and not enough time assessing whether the other person desires our destination.

Perhaps you disagree. Perhaps you think The Magic "If" won't work.

Maybe you're right. But *if* it might work more often with more people, would you be willing to try it with the next three people you speak with?

Maybe it won't work for you. *If* it could make you a more persuasive libertarian, would you want it?

# The Reverse

Tired of long, drawn-out arguments about government? Worn out from explaining why government fails and makes things worse?

What if you could convince your listener to persuade *himself* about libertarianism? What if you could persuade him to marshall compelling and convincing evidence and arguments that would change his own mind about libertarianism?

Persuade himself? How?

The Reverse.

Instead of telling him what's right with liberty and wrong with government, ask him, "What's one thing that government does now that you think it definitely should *not* do?"

Or: "What's one activity that government engages in that it should stop doing?"

Or: "What's one government program that's a dismal failure or a waste of money that government ought to shut down?"

Then ask, "Why?"

After he tells you why, ask him to tell you more. Ask him to elaborate and expand. To tell you about the consequences of the bad program. To give you examples.

Then play Devil's Advocate. Ask him how he would respond to possible objections. "Suppose someone said X, how would you answer that objection?" "Suppose someone said Y, how would you answer that objection?"

He will argue himself into a libertarian position. And will give you the evidence and arguments that are most convincing to him.

The Reverse lets your listener pick the part of government

that he's most opposed to, do your arguing for you, and it intensifies his opposition.

How and why does it work?

It begins with what your listener already believes. It respects his beliefs and values.

It creates rapport. Agreement. You both agree that government should abandon this activity or program.

As Pascal wrote, "We are usually convinced more easily by reasons we have found ourselves than by those which have occurred to others."

As Win Wenger writes in *The Einstein Factor:* "The sheer act of expressing our thoughts on some subject causes us to learn more about that subject, even when no new information has been provided from without."

Why does The Reverse work?

To truly learn a subject, teach it.

To help our listeners learn, we must ask them to teach.

# The Assisted Suicide Request

"What are the three biggest misconceptions that people have about libertarians?" asks the reporter.

"What are the three worst accusations that people make about libertarians?" asks the talk show host.

"What are the three most negative things that people say about libertarians?" asks the caller.

*Warning:* If you answer the question you are requesting assisted suicide... for libertarianism.

Newspaper reporters, talk radio hosts, TV interviewers, and Devil's Advocate questioners sometimes offer assisted political suicide to those who answer the question.

If you provide misconceptions or accusations or negative beliefs... reporters will lead the article with them, talk radio hosts will dwell upon them, and questioners will assume that where there's smoke, there's fire.

Imagine headlines or lead paragraphs that begin with:

"Libertarians deny they're anarchists..."

"Libertarians are accused of being mean and selfish, but they say..."

"People believe that libertarians are callous and indifferent to the suffering of those less fortunate, but libertarians say..."

"Will libertarians put heroin vending machines and prostitution in your community? No, say Libertarian Party leaders, who complain..."

Do you find yourself defending libertarianism against the charges you raised?

Stop answering the assisted political suicide request!

Answer positively and persuasively:

1. **Full version**: "Most people are unfamiliar with libertarian ideas. The national Libertarian Party commissioned a poll after the 1996 Presidential campaign to determine how many people know who the Libertarian Presidential candidate was. The pollsters offered 20 names to the people polled. Only 4% said: 'Harry Browne.' Ninety-six percent of the American people had no idea who the Libertarian Presidential candidate was — or what libertarians believe. Libertarians believe in individual liberty and full personal responsibility. Libertarians believe in dramatically smaller government now. Libertarians believe that every person should be self-governing."

2. **Short version**: "Most Americans don't know much about libertarians and libertarian ideas. 'Libertarian' comes from the root word 'liberty.' Libertarians believe in individual liberty and personal responsibility. Libertarians want to dramatically shrink the size and power of government — and limit it to the protection of our life, liberty, and property."

3. **Shorter version**: "Most people I talk with have very positive impressions about libertarianism and libertarians. They realize that libertarians stand for individual liberty and personal responsibility... for the Declaration of Independence and the Constitution and the Statue of Liberty."

Give positive answers to negative questions.

When they ask about our flaws and weaknesses, showcase our strengths.

When they ask for shadows, shine the light of liberty.

# Why Are Some Libertarians So Negative?

"I love liberty, but I don't like some libertarians," said the man across the table from me.

"You must have a good reason for feeling that way. What is it that you dislike about some libertarians?" I asked.

"They're too negative. They're always complaining about taxes or government spending or government programs or politicians. They blame government for just about everything that's wrong. They tell me how awful government is. And every time I talk with them, they play the same old broken record: 'Government is always wrong, government is evil, government is the enemy,'" said the man.

The man has a point. Some libertarians fill conversations with the failures and flaws, the costs and consequences, the errors and evils of government.

And that's all they talk about.

Their friends and co-workers cringe when they start ranting and railing and raving against anything and everything the government does.

They are boo-leaders. Misery merchants. Gloom and doomers. Bearers of bad news.

They foment frustration and anger and hate.

They darken the rooms they enter. They pollute conversations with spiritual toxic waste.

Their friends and families and co-workers silently suffer at first... then they stop listening.

Perhaps you know one of these nega-tarians.

How can you help them become persuasive and positive?

Should you ask them to stop talking about the destructive

impact of government programs and policies?

Or maybe compromise and water down what they believe? Praise government?

None of the above. Neither negativity, nor compromise, nor silence, nor surrender.

Why not recommend a persuasive libertarian approach:
1. Diagnose the disease and describe its dangers.
2. Recommend our remedy.
3. Spell out its strengths.

For example:
1. The minimum wage throws inner-city African Americans and other minorities out of work. It prevents them from getting badly-needed job experience. It keeps them from auditioning for higher-paying jobs. The minimum wage keeps them from grabbing the bottom rung of the economic latter.
2. End the minimum wage and let untrained and un-skilled workers start at low-paying jobs so they can develop job skills, create job histories, and demonstrate that they deserve higher wages and promotions.
3. Removing the minimum wage barrier lets new workers begin their climb up the earnings ladder. It lets them climb as fast and far as their work ethic and skills develop. The small business that can't afford a $7-an-hour dishwasher can afford a $4-an-hour dishwasher. And the dishwasher can earn while he learns... to be a waiter or cook. Without a lower bottom rung, he'd never get on the ladder.

If we do not diagnose the disease, no one will feel they want or need the remedy.

If we *only* diagnose the disease... and spend all evening telling our listeners how awful it is... and how soon the undertaker will come calling, we'll be one of those negative libertarians.

We must briefly diagnose and describe, then fully recommend the remedy and rewards.

We need only briefly sketch out the harmful government program, and lay out the high costs and bad consequences.

Then we must emphasize our libertarian solution, and the benefits it brings.

We must accentuate the positives of a free market and very

small, limited government, the blessings of personal responsibility and individual liberty, and the strengths of self-governing individuals.

We must describe and dramatize the direct, personal benefits of our libertarian solutions.

We must promote positive libertarianism.

# "What Kind of a Conservative Are You?"

One evening, over 20 years ago, I fell into a conversation about politics at a party. Everyone had opinions about politics. One man sat quietly for half an hour, then announced to everyone, "I think you're all wrong. You don't understand standards and decency and authority. I do. I'm a conservative." Two of my fellow libertarians started rebutting "conservatism" and accusing this man of holding false beliefs.

He responded to the criticisms — and attacked libertarianism for condoning "license."

The libertarians were counter-attacking, when I interrupted the argument by shouting, "Wait a minute. I'm confused. I need some help here. Could you straighten me out on something?"

Everyone quieted down. I spoke to the conservative.

"What kind of a conservative are you?" I asked. "I've read a lot of conservative writers and met a lot of conservatives, and I've noticed that there are several different kinds of conservatives. There are fiscal conservatives, whose main concern is that government live within its means. There are social conservatives, who want government to enforce a strict morality. There are nationalist conservatives, who want to restrict trade and immigration and fight those who oppose the American way of life. Are you primarily a fiscal conservative, a social conservative, or a nationalist conservative? What kind of a conservative are you?"

"Well, I'm mainly a fiscal conservative," he said.

"Are you a big-government fiscal conservative or a small-government fiscal conservative? Do you want a big and powerful government that lives within its means or a small and limited government that lives within its means?" I asked.

"Are you kidding? Government is way too big. I want a small, constitutionally limited government," he responded.

We had a great discussion on which federal agencies he'd abolish and where he'd slash government and why.

We went from an escalating argument to an interesting, friendly discussion. This small-government fiscal conservative and three libertarians found we had a lot in common.

And it began with asking him what he did believe and what he did not. By not assuming that all conservatives are the same.

Suppose that someone said, "I'm a Christian." Should we assume that all Christians are the same?

Or should we ask, "What kind of a Christian are you, Catholic or Protestant? What denomination are you: Methodist, Lutheran, Baptist, Pentecostal, Seventh-day Adventist, Quaker...? Could you tell me a little bit about your faith? What do you have in common with other Christians — and how are you different?"

If someone says, "I'm a liberal," we can ask:

"What kind of a liberal are you? What are your liberal beliefs? What do you have in common with other liberals — and how are you different? Are you a central-planning liberal or a grassroots, community decision-making liberal? Are you a civil-liberties liberal or a government-without-limits liberal?"

If someone says, "I'm a socialist," we can ask:

"What kind of a socialist are you? Small communes and communities... or centrally planned in Washington, DC? Are you a coercive socialist or a voluntary socialist? Could someone choose *not* to participate in your socialism?"

Before we can honestly say, "I agree" or "I disagree," we must understand. To understand, we must ask. With courtesy and interest and a sincere desire to learn the truth.

We may discover that they disagree with us.

We may discover that we have a lot in common. That they agree with us on many important things. And that we may be able to persuade them on other things. Isn't that worth seeking?

What kind of a communicator are you?

Are you one who assumes, or one who asks? Are you one who wants to shoot first and ask questions later, or one who sincerely wants to understand?

What kind of communicator are you?

# The Six-Step Recipe for Cooking Big Government

"There are over 40 million Americans without adequate health care insurance. Shouldn't the government do something?" asks the questioner.

"Fifteen years from now, we'll have another 60 million Americans ready to retire. Social Security needs more funds. Shouldn't government do something?" asks another.

"Public schools are failing. We need more money to educate our kids. Shouldn't the federal government do something?" asks a third.

You've heard these questions. And dozens like them.

Responding directly often makes it look like libertarians are against the positive intentions behind the programs — or against the people who depend on the programs.

We may look like the Grinch who stole kindness.

We don't have to stand there and look bad.

Because I have a six-step recipe that cooks the Big Government approach — and sets the table for freedom.

Let's use the first question to illustrate the six steps.

"There are over 40 million Americans without adequate health care insurance. Shouldn't the government do something?" asks the questioner.

**Step 1: Empathize with his positive intentions:**

"It's awful when Americans who are sick or injured find themselves without medical care. We don't want to stand by while others suffer. We need to do something positive. Something that makes things better..." (Even though the question says "health insurance," the person's intention is that these people get health *care*.)

As sales trainer Cavett Robert wrote in 1962, "No one cares how much you know — until they know how much you care."

**Step 2: "Big Government programs don't work."**

Give examples of program failures from *Healing Our World* by Mary Ruwart, or *Losing Ground* by Charles Murray, or *Why Government Doesn't Work* by Harry Browne.

**Step 3: "Big Government programs often make things worse for the very people they're intended to help."**

Offer examples of things that were made worse, from the books above or from James Bovard's books or from any one of dozens listed in the Laissez Faire Books catalog.

**Step 4: "Big Government programs create new problems."**

Use examples of the new problems from the books above or from *The Tragedy of American Compassion* by Marvin Olasky or *Reclaiming the American Dream* by Richard C. Cornuelle.

**Step 5: "Big Government programs are wasteful and costly."**

Offer examples from James Bovard or the books above or "Talking Points" in *Libertarian Party News* or from one of John Stossel's reports on *20/20* — or from the *Liberator Online's* "Good News, Bad News, Unbelievable News" by James W. Harris.

**Step 6: "Big Government programs divert money and energy from positive and productive uses."**

You may want to use free-market success stories, or refer to one of the many fine articles in *Reason* magazine.

Or you may want to ask your questioner, "How do you think you and I, working with our churches or service organizations like the Lions Club or the Rotary Club or local businesses, might help solve this problem in our community? If the government didn't take all of that money from us in high taxes, if the government didn't get in the way, how could we solve this problem locally?"

This six-step recipe cooks the Big Government approach to dealing with social problems. And it clears the way for discussing libertarian solutions to social problems.

1. Empathy.
2. Government programs don't work.
3. Government programs often make things worse for those they intend to help.

4. Government programs create new problems.
5. Government programs are wasteful and costly.
6. Government programs divert money from more positive and productive uses.

This approach requires that we become well-informed about the harms of Big Government — and the benefits and blessings of individual liberty, personal responsibility, and small government.

This is the recipe, not the dinner. You need to shop for the ingredients yourself. You need to familiarize yourself with libertarian and free-market magazines, newsletters, books, and tapes.

This approach does not show how and why a free society will solve these problems.

This approach shows how and why Big Government programs have not, do not, and cannot solve our problems.

When we're moving in the wrong direction, we don't want to go further or faster.

We must turn around.

And head toward blue skies and open roads.

Toward freedom.

# Are You Tied in Nots?

"Libertarians are not anarchists," responded the Libertarian.

"Libertarians do not condone drugs," said another.

"Libertarians do not support license," answered yet another.

The statements are true. But they often reinforce the falsehood.

Why?

They tie us in Nots. The "not" ties us to the false accusations.

"Not" is a language tool, a linguistic device. It negates what it refers to.

To understand a "notted" sentence, you need to focus on what is being negated. And that is what is remembered.

They remember the subject, verb, and object. Intensely. And the negation... barely.

Try this:

"Jones is not an evil person. Jones did not lie and cheat and steal. It has not been proved that Jones is sick and depraved and wicked. Not one shred of evidence indicates that Jones underhandedly conned widows and orphans out of their life savings."

People remember the name and the charge. The accusations. They remember "Jones... evil person" and "Jones... lie, cheat, and steal."

To deny, we must assert. To negate, we must affirm.

To communicate what libertarians *are*, we must communicate positively. For others to remember what libertarians *advocate*, we must communicate what we are *for*.

What are we *for*? "Libertarians advocate small government."

What do we advocate? "Libertarians want to end the insane

War on Drugs."

What do we believe? "Libertarians are committed to personal responsibility... because personal responsibility is the price of liberty."

Notted: "Libertarians do not believe in the initiation of the use of force." (Will be remembered as "Libertarians... initiation of force.")

Un-notted: "Libertarians believe that all human dealings should be voluntary."

Notted: "Libertarians are not callous toward the poor." (Will be remembered as "Libertarians... callous toward the poor.")

Un-notted: "Libertarians support charity toward the weak and frail and poor."

Notted: "Libertarians would not support military intervention in other countries." (Will be remembered as "Libertarians... military intervention.")

Un-notted: "Libertarians believe that our military should defend our American shores and soil against foreign invaders."

Notted sentences reinforce the belief being negated.

Notted sentences often confuse.

Notted sentences are defensive.

Notted sentences are often weak.

Say what we are for, not not for. (Did that jangle or confuse you?)

Advocate, do not negate. (Did that tweak you?)

Say what we *do* believe. Not what we do not.

Affirm what we *will* do. Not what we will not.

Cut the not.

Say it positively to communicate it clearly.

So others will remember what libertarians are for.

# The Wrong End of the Stick

"I agree that 20,000 gun control laws is way too many," the interviewer said to me. "Which gun laws would you leave on the books?"

"Yes, government is too big," said my talk radio caller. "But what parts of the federal government would libertarians leave intact?"

"Taxes are too high," a conservative agreed. "But we can't just abolish taxes. Which taxes should we keep?"

There are many positive ways to respond to these questions. But there's something interesting afoot here. All the questions rest upon one basic question: "Which parts of government do libertarians support and condone?"

Or: "From a libertarian standpoint, which functions of government are right or good, moral, or practical?"

This is theoretically interesting. Philosophically important.

But when we enter into this discussion, we're reaching for... The Wrong End of the Stick.

Rather than find areas of *disagreement* on which gun laws to keep, which parts of government to leave intact, or which taxes to keep.... we should look for *agreement* on which gun laws to repeal, which parts of government to remove, and which taxes to rescind.

Rather than argue over what is or is not a proper function of government, let's agree what is *definitely not.*

Rather than focus on disagreements over what parts of government to leave, let us focus on agreements of what parts absolutely, positively must go.

On gun laws, I responded, "20,000 gun laws is a lot to sort

through. If it were up to you, which one would you get rid of first? Which anti-gun law do you think is most harmful? And why?"

On Big Government, I answered, "We agree that government is way too big. Which part of Big Government do you think is worst? Why? If it were your choice, would you remove it? Why?"

On taxes, I responded, "What's the worst thing about high taxes? Why? If it were your decision, and your decision alone, which tax would you repeal or cut? How much would you cut it? Why?"

The right end of the stick is:

"Which parts of Big Government should we erase now?"

"Which activities of government are wrong or bad, immoral, or impractical?"

"Which government program causes the most harm? Which government policy is the most destructive?"

"What is government doing that it definitely should *not* do?"

We can reach for either end of the stick.

One end gives us a tug-of-war.

The other end gives us a helping hand.

Reach for the Right End of The Stick.

# Would You Push the Button?

"We didn't get into the War on Drugs overnight," said the talk radio show caller. "And we won't get out of it overnight. It may take years to wind down the War on Drugs."

"You may be right," I responded. "But let's try an experiment. If there were a button in front of you, and by pushing that button, you could immediately end the War on Drugs... would you push the button?"

Ten seconds of dead air. Silence. Every talk radio host's enemy.

"Yes, I would," my caller said. "I would push the button."

"Why? Why would you push the button?" I asked.

"Because the War on Drugs is a failure. You can get any kind of drug you want. Drugs are everywhere. Who's kidding who?" he answered.

Sometimes libertarians get caught up in arguments over transition programs, over how to wind down and sunset destructive government programs. Or how fast to phase them out.

Sometimes these discussions are important. Often they are not.

The "push the button" test gets to the heart of the matter. It clears the air.

"If there were a button in front of you, and by pushing that button, you could totally privatize Social Security, get it entirely out of the hands of government, would you push the button?"

"If there were a button in front of you, and by pushing that button you could immediately repeal all 20,000 anti-gun laws, immediately restore the right to keep and bear arms, would you push the button?"

"If there were a button in front of you, and by pushing that button, you could make the government so small it didn't need an income tax, would you push the button?"

It's simple. Personal. Concrete. Memorable.

Here's the recipe. Ask the person who's uncertain:

1. "If there were a button in front of you, and by pushing that button, you could immediately repeal/end/remove [government program or law], would you push the button?"

2. If they say yes, ask, "Why?" As Blaise Pascal observed, "We are generally the better persuaded by reasons we discover ourselves than by those given to us by others."

3. "How would things be dramatically different or better if you pushed the button? What would be the biggest and best benefits?"

4. "How else would we directly and immediately profit from ending this thing?"

If there were a question you could ask, and by asking that question you could help people get to the core of liberty, would you ask that question?

Would you push that button?

&ast; &ast; &ast;

Note: I learned the "Push the Button" question in 1973 from Leonard Read of the Foundation for Economic Education.

# Thirsty Horses

"Why couldn't you convince that guy that libertarianism is right?" asked John.

"You can lead a horse to water, but you can't make him drink," said Bill, a new libertarian.

Sometimes that's true. Other times, it's an excuse. Often, it's an opportunity to learn.

Let's consider the horse that would not drink.

Maybe he wasn't thirsty. Maybe he didn't like our water. Maybe he didn't like the way you lead him to the stream.

You might have the wrong horse.

Or maybe we're asking the wrong questions. Maybe we're trying to solve the wrong problem.

We're trying to figure our why this one horse won't drink our water.

We need thirsty horses.

How do we find thirsty horses? When we lead thirsty horses to water, they'll drink as much as they can.

How can we tell when a horse is thirsty? How does he act? How does he look? What are the clues?

How can I tell when a horse is not thirsty? How is he different from a thirsty horse?

How can I make horses thirsty? As infomercial pioneer Steve Scott suggests, "Salt their oats... and they'll drink as much water as you want."

How can I motivate horses to come to me when they are thirsty?

How can I get horses that can't or won't drink to lead me to thirsty horses?

How can I make my water more attractive to horses that are thirsty?

Too many frustrated libertarians blame the horse. They hold his head under until he drinks or drowns.

When it comes to persuasion, libertarians need more horse sense.

We try to persuade people who don't want liberty... that they do want it.

We need to find people who want the blessings and benefits of liberty.

*        *        *

How do we find thirsty prospects? Ask prospects if they're thirsty.

"Do you think government is too big, about the right size, or too small?"

"Do you think taxes are too low, about the right amount, or too high?"

"Do you have too much freedom, about the right amount of freedom, or too little freedom?

Reach out to them when they feel the heavy hand of government. April 15th. In line at the Department of Motor Vehicles. When they have just received an IRS audit notice. When they pay their property taxes. Or after they paid taxes on their parents' estate.

Reach out to them when someone they deeply care about is feeling government's heavy hand. A son or a daughter arrested for smoking marijuana. A neighbor or family member who is being audited by the IRS. A friend with a business or rental property that is being hounded by government bureaucrats.

*        *        *

How can we tell when a prospect is thirsty? What are the clues?

Offer them water. "If we could have a federal government so small it didn't need an income tax, would you want it?" "If it were possible to end Drug Prohibition and the no-win, morally wrong War on Drugs, would you want it?" "If it were possible to repeal all 20,000 anti-gun laws, would you want it?"

Listen to them. "That bleepity-bleep federal government is too $@#% bossy!" "Can you believe these $%@*!$# taxes?" "Did you see *Mr. Stossel goes to Washington?* It was really cool." (If the person is complaining about government or politicians, chances are, they're thirsty.

*       *       *

How can I tell when a prospect is not thirsty? How is he different from a thirsty prospect?

Listen to them. If they never complain about government, politicians, or taxes, they probably aren't thirsty. Nor if they praise the government for doing the best it can.

If they proudly work for the government. A happy IRS auditor. A self-righteous DEA agent. A Department of Motor Vehicles employee who believes the people in line are an imposition.

If they *tell* you they're not thirsty. Especially if you've offered them water on a dozen previous occasions.

*       *       *

How can I make prospects thirsty? Steven K. Scott's *A Millionaire's Notebook* teaches two techniques. A. Salt their oats. B. Emotional word pictures.

How do you salt their oats? How do you make them thirsty? What's the secret to getting them to ask you to lead them to water? You just experienced three examples. Questions! What thought-provoking questions can you ask that will stimulate their interest in liberty? What questions would intrigue or hook them? What questions would prompt them to say, "Tell me more"? What questions about government or liberty would tempt or tantalize them?

(Does this intrigue you enough to go test your salt questions on unsuspecting and possibly thirsty horses? Does this tempt you enough to go looking for horses?)

"An emotional word picture is a statement or story that enables the hearer to visualize what is being said," writes Steven Scott.

Use emotional word picture techniques from some of the other chapters in this book: The Better Mousetrap Myth, Welfare Pigeons, The Other Person's Shoes, Persuasion Lessons from the Gardener, Flat Earth Politics, Evangelist or Church Preacher, The Wrong End of the Stick, Prospecting For Gold, Would You Push the Button?, Big Government As Wile E. Coyote, Take Out the Trash, Chinese Bamboo, and Ben Franklin's Road to Excellence.

Aesop's Fables. The parables of Jesus. Tales from Uncle Remus. Fairy tales and fables.

*          *          *

How can I motivate prospects to come to me when they *are* thirsty?

Advertise and publicize your water.

Create word-of-mouth. Tell everybody how thirst-quenching your water is.

Hand out road maps that show people how to get to your water. (For example, steer them to the Advocates for Self-Government's Web site at www.TheAdvocates.org.)

When they are thirsty, point them to your water. You don't have to motivate them. Their thirst will motivate them.

*          *          *

How can I get prospects who can't or won't drink to lead me to thirsty horses?

Ask them to do it. "It sounds to me like you're not interested in my libertarian ideas. If you have a friend or co-worker who is interested, would you ask them to get in touch with me?" Or: "Would you give me their phone number or email address?"

Show them how to tell when a horse is thirsty.

*          *          *

How can I make my water more attractive to horses that are thirsty?

Don't quench their thirst with a fire hose. Don't make them drink more than they want.

Don't muddy the water. Don't put things in the stream that have nothing to do with water. Your opinions on religion, or sex, or how to raise children do not belong in the water. Your personal values do not belong in the water. The water belongs in the water.

Make it safe to drink there. Don't brow-beat or threaten a prospect sampling our libertarian ideas. Let them decide how thirsty they are, and when they want to return.

*          *          *

There's nothing wrong with the horses.

There's nothing wrong with the water.

To persuade we must master the subject of thirst.

# What to Do When You Don't Know or Don't Understand

"As was demonstrated in a recent scientific study of the American Society of Pediatricians, when guns are kept in the home, boys will find them, and boys will play with those guns. Loaded handguns!" said the speaker. "As they proved, the only way to keep children from dying from handguns is to get rid of handguns. Are you going to face the facts or hold on to your prejudice that guns are no danger to our children?"

How would you answer this? What would you say?

When confronted with new information — or mis-information — most of us pretend that we already know it. Pretend that we are familiar with the facts. We fake it.

Why?

For most of us, admitting ignorance is admitting weakness. Confessing to a flaw. Pleading guilty to the sin of not knowing.

"If you understand the parameters of the impact made by the multiplier effect on economic disequilibrium, in conjunction with misaligned supply-demand curves, with the M-2 money supply as the critical variable, you'll realize why price caps on energy resources in California can assist short-term misallocations and clearing functions," said the TV political pundit.

When confronted with complicated or convoluted statements, most of us nod our heads and try to look like we understand. We say, "I see." Or "Uh-huh."

Why?

For most of us, admitting confusion is admitting that we are flawed. Ill-informed. Maybe even on the wrong end of the bell curve.

Ignorance and confusion. They challenge our intelligence. Our thinking skills.

But mostly, they challenge our egos. Our courage. Our honesty. Can we admit we don't know? Can we admit we are confused?

Because ignorance and confusion are doorways to learning. I know. Because I kept these doors locked for many years. Out of embarrassment. Shame. Fear of looking like a fool. Feelings of stupidity and incompetence.

I'm not a saint in admitting ignorance or confusion. I'm a recovering sinner.

Here's what I've learned.

When I don't know something, I say, "I don't know."

When I don't understand something, I say, "I don't understand." Or, "I don't get it."

When I'm confused, I say, "I'm confused."

Admitting ignorance or confusion is the first step. The second step is to ask for help. For example: "Would you tell me where I could find that study by the American Society of Pediatricians?"

"Would you explain it to me?"

"Could you give me an example?"

"Would you show me how it works?"

"Could you walk me through it, step by step?"

Or: "I'm not familiar with some of these phrases. What's a 'multiplier effect'? Could you give me a couple of examples? How does it work? What does the phrase 'economic disequilibrium' mean? What's a 'misaligned supply-demand curve'? Or the 'M-2 money supply'? What are the consequences of a price cap? What's a 'short-term misallocation'? What are 'clearing functions'?"

"You're smart. You understand it. Could you make this simple enough for me to understand?"

"Explain it to me like I'm a 12-year-old kid. Make it clear enough for a bright child."

"I'm confused. Could you straighten me out on this?"

Don't be surprised if the other person stutters, stammers, or stumbles. Sometimes he's as ignorant and confused as we are. But he was too embarrassed to ask. So he repeated what he didn't understand.

We may have to study the subject together.

Sometimes he'll stop and think. He may well understand it, but need to figure out how to simplify it. Or clarify it. So he can clearly communicate it to us.

Sometimes, he'll stop and realize that he was wrong. Simplifying it, clarifying it, and explaining it may lead him to rejecting it. Which is what would happen to anyone who examined the incompetently designed, unscientific gun "study" done by American Society of Pediatricians.

It's still hard for me to admit when I'm ignorant and confused. But each time I do, I learn a great deal. And so do those I talk with.

# The Power Pause

Have you ever watched *Hannity and Colmes? The O'Reilly Factor? Hardball with Chris Matthews? Crossfire?*
They're supposed to bring us political debate. Dialogue. Discussion.
They offer us an exchange of monologues, not dialogues.
One person talking with the other waiting to talk. Neither listening to the other. Neither considering the ideas and information of the other.
This is a caricature of conversation. A parody of discussion. A mockery of people reasoning with one another.
It's an exaggeration of what sometimes happens when people discuss ideas. We can't wait to talk. So we don't listen.
We can't wait to get in a word edgewise. So we don't let the other person get a word in either.
We need to stop, look, and listen. We need to pause.
We need to pause to consider what the other person said.
Pause and reflect. Pause and let the other person's ideas affect and influence us.
The pause has power.
When you pause before you speak, the other person's attention level goes up.
When you pause before your respond, you let the other person know you're reflecting on what he just said. That you respect him and his ideas.
A pause gives you time to choose your next question, your next statement, your next response.
A pause lets you choose which path to take the conversation down.

A pause lets you interrupt unproductive exchanges. Stop the toxic process from continuing. Halt the harmful momentum. A pause punctuates conversation, just as a rest punctuates music.

A pause lets you step back and gain perspective. It gives you new choices. New possibilities. Some people pause... then they speak.

Some people hold an index finger up, and say, "Just a minute, I'm thinking over what you said." Pause... then they speak. Pause to listen. Pause to punctuate. Pause for power. Pause to let them listen. To you. To themselves.

Pause to slow the conversation down. Sometimes you have to slow down discussions to speed up understanding.

You can pause for dramatic effect. You can pause for pragmatic effect... as a practical way to stop the conversation from barreling on in the wrong direction.

A pause is a conversational tool. An under-used tool.

Pause for power. Pause for understanding. Pause for a meeting of minds.

# The Turnaround

"Ms. Howell, won't ending the income tax in Massachusetts cripple the state government?" asked the newspaper reporter. "The Massachusetts income tax cripples family budgets," responded Carla Howell. "Massachusetts Big Government cripples our businesses, cripples our charities, and cripples our churches. Massachusetts Big Government and the income tax cripple our ability to support our families and help our neighbors."

"Mr. Cloud, isn't your ballot initiative to end the income tax simply appealing to each taxpayer's personal greed?" asked the talk radio host.

"Ever-growing, greedy government in Massachusetts takes and takes and takes," I answered. "Every year, greedy state government takes more and more and more. Government tax greed is insatiable. Year after year, government demands ever-increasing taxes from the working people in our state. Say 'No' to government tax greed. Say 'Yes' to ending the income tax in Massachusetts."

Each question was an accusation.

Each question asserted that those who want to end the income tax are selfish, greedy, callous, stingy, mean-spirited, and willing to inflict pain and suffering on others.

The assumptions are not simply false: they are the opposite of the truth.

The accusations reveal the secret sins of the accusers.

Private citizens are tax producers. Government is a tax consumer.

Most TV news reporters and newspaper reporters have a

pro-Big Government bias. Their questions are based on the unquestioned belief that Big Government programs are necessary and good.

But if Big Government programs are necessary and good, then those who oppose them must be — bad, vicious, and cruel. So it's understandable that news reporters ask the questions they do.

And if we libertarians allow news reporters or opinion columnists or other supporters of Big Government to frame the discussion and debate this way, we'll always be on the defensive.

We must turn the tables on the accusers.

We must use The Turnaround.

It's simple and easy to use.

Let's say that we're proposing a tax repeal or tax cut, a government spending reduction, or rolling back or ending a Big Government program.

The Big Government-biased question will often be something like this:

"Won't your proposal deprive government of desperately needed dollars?" Or: "Won't this bankrupt a shaky state budget?" Or: "Won't this hurt government's ability to help the needy?"

Take the accusatory words — "deprive... desperately needed... bankrupt... hurt" — and use them in several assertions *against* the government. Turn around the accusations. Apply them to the government.

For example, "Massachusetts Big Government deprives working families of desperately-needed dollars. The Massachusetts income tax deprives taxpayers of the dollars they desperately need to support their churches and charities. Our state government deprives families of the dollars they desperately need for the baby on the way, the roof that won't last another winter, or the car that needs repairs to make it through another year."

The Turnaround gives *you* the initiative.

The Turnaround reframes the issue.

The Turnaround is recyclable. You can use it again and again.

The Turnaround exposes the reporter and the audience to a new possibility: libertarianism.

# Turbocharge with Benefits

Want to try a fun communication experiment? Turn on one of the popular TV shows that discuss and debate current events and issues. *The O'Reilly Factor. Hardball with Chris Matthews. Hannity and Colmes. Meet the Press. Face the Nation. Crossfire.* Write down the issue or event being discussed. Write down the guest's name and the guest's position on the issue.

Now list the major points the guest makes to advance or defend his position. When the segment is over, review the points he made. Circle any point that highlighted a benefit.

I tried this experiment with four shows one evening. The results? Four shows, three hours, and only two benefits mentioned.

Their guests were smart, knowledgeable, and well-spoken. They covered their talking points. They told us what they believed and why. Yet they failed to persuade.

Why? They failed to show us the *benefits* of their positions and proposals. They failed to show us how and where and why we would be better off with their remedy.

It's a common mistake. Even prominent libertarians will make a powerful case against Social Security, a powerful case for getting pensions and retirement entirely out of the hands of government, and then... fail to sketch out the three or four biggest benefits of our libertarian approach.

Even bright, well-read libertarians will marshal a compelling case for ending the no-win, morally wrong War on Drugs, and then... fail to spotlight the three or four most powerful benefits of our libertarian proposal.

Libertarian speakers will present airtight theoretical arguments and empirical evidence for separating school and state, and then... neglect the three or four huge, immediate, direct benefits of our libertarian remedy.

Libertarians will cite great books like *More Guns, Less Crime* and *The 7 Myths of Gun Control*... demolish anti-gun propaganda, and demonstrate the injury and damage caused by the war on guns, and then... fail to illustrate the three or four immense benefits of ending the war on guns.

Why? We get caught up in our evidence and arguments, caught up in our proofs and positions, and forget to "show them the money."

We know the benefits, but forget to *show* the benefits.

The solution? A benefit phrase. At the end of your case, right after you offer your libertarian position or proposal, add one of the following phrases:

1. "...and here's what this means to you... [name three or four benefits]."
2. "...and here's what this does for you... [list three or four benefits]."
3. "...and here are three ways that this benefits you: [list]."
4. "There are three major benefits to my proposal. They are... [list]."

Some people are more concerned about your proposal helping those they deeply care about than whether the proposal helps them. This is often the key with parents and grandparents.

For example, "...and here's what ending the War on Drugs will mean to your children... There will be no obscene profits for pushing drugs to your children, no drug gangs trying to recruit them, and if, in spite of the best you can do, one of your kids gets involved with drugs, he'll have every opportunity to stop using, with the help of family and friends, rather than being sentenced to 10 or 20 years in prison. A better world for your children. Isn't that what you want?"

Benefits sell liberty.

Benefits persuade people to explore and embrace our ideas.

Benefits turbocharge our libertarian communication.

So, talk benefits.

And here's what talking benefits will mean to you...

# Are You Skipping the Last Step in Persuasion?

The War on Drugs and Drug Prohibition. You've finally convinced your best friend that these programs are destructive and morally wrong. He finally agrees with you. Are you done?

The war on guns. It took a lot of reading, research, and conversation — from *More Guns, Less Crime* by John Lott to *The 7 Myths of Gun Control* by Richard Poe — but you persuaded your brother or sister to embrace the cause of gun freedom. You agree. Are you done?

Big Government. You powerfully presented the Five Iron Laws of Big Government, had a lively and fun conversation comparing and contrasting Big Government with small government, and now your co-worker is convinced. You agree. Are you done?

No. If you stop with agreement, you've quit too soon.

If you stop persuading when people say they agree, they'll relapse to Big Government thinking. Quickly if they watch TV news, read newspapers, or socialize and work with people who talk about politics and current events. Slowly if they don't read or think or talk about politics and current events.

Why? Because we're influenced by the TV news we watch, by the newspapers we read, by the people we talk with.

Most of these people went to government-run public schools. Which teach Big Government thinking. Which teach that government can and does solve social problems.

"What should government do?" is their first thought. Because they were taught to think this way in government-run public schools.

And so were their brothers and sisters, their friends and neighbors, and virtually everyone else they know. Not to mention the people who report the news to them.

When a cucumber gets tossed into a vat of brine, the brine does not get cucumbered, the cucumber gets pickled. Environment is relentless. Fast or slow, completely or partially, it influences and changes us.

If agreement is fragile, what is the last step in persuasion? Action.

After someone agrees, we must persuade them to *act* on behalf of the new belief.

A small first step may be enough. Because a small step leads to another small step. Then another. Then to a larger step. Many an avalanche started with one small snowball.

Persuade them to take action. Any action that moves them forward to greater knowledge and greater involvement.

Persuade them to act. Get them to subscribe to the *Liberator Online*. Appeal for action. Get them to become an active volunteer or donor to a libertarian organization or project. Ask them to act. Get them to buy a libertarian book from Laissez Faire Books.

Action leads to more action and involvement. More positive exposure to libertarianism.

Persuasion requires understanding. Then agreement. Then action. Persuading them to take action may be your last step of the persuasion process.

But action is their first step. Toward becoming a libertarian.

✻　　✻　　✻

## The Five Iron Laws of Big Government
*by Michael Cloud*

I.   Big Government programs don't work.
II.  Big Government programs make things worse, often hurting the very people they are intended to help.
III. Big Government programs create new problems.
IV.  Big Government programs are costly and wasteful.
V.   Big Government programs divert money and energy from positive, productive uses.

# The Stunning Impact of Simple Questions

"You're trying to over-simplify an extremely complicated political issue, Mr. Cloud," charged my National Public Radio interviewer.

"Quite the opposite. You are over-complicating a political issue that we can resolve with a few simple questions," I responded. "I have five questions that should clear this up. Let's put them on the table — and discuss them one by one. Okay?"

I laid out the questions. We went through them one by one. The NPR host found himself at a loss — not for words, but for ideas or answers.

The radio host had a huge number of political assumptions that he had never examined. So do most people.

"The unexamined life is not worth living," said Socrates. So, too, with unexamined beliefs and assumptions.

"Examine your premises," wrote Ayn Rand.

Examine your key libertarian concepts, principles, and premises. Break down each one. Take each one apart. Does it make sense? Is it valid or true? What are three examples of it?

Can you make each key libertarian concept, principle, or premise understandable to a 12-year-old? Can you explain its meaning, implications, and applications simply enough that the 12-year-old could explain it to his friends?

Try this with a few key libertarian ideas.

1. What's a libertarian?
2. What is individual liberty?
3. What is personal responsibility?
4. What is small government?
5. What is ownership? What is property? What are

property rights?
6. What are voluntary human relations? How are they different from the initiation of force? In plain and simple words, what do these phrases mean? What are three examples of each? Write out a few different simple answers to each question. It'll improve your libertarian thinking and conversations. You'll become a confident libertarian communicator.

After you've clarified and simplified your own libertarian ideas, then you're ready to explore the stunning impact of simple questions with Big Government ideas and assumptions. Consider one example:

"I believe in collective responsibility, *not* personal responsibility," wrote one Massachusetts liberal. Then she proposed several Big Government policies and programs.

I wrote back, "I'm not sure I understand you. Could you please help me out with a few pointers?

"What do you mean by the phrase 'collective responsibility'?

"Would you give me a few examples of collective responsibility — and how it works?

"Is each person free to choose or refuse collective responsibility? Is it voluntary or mandatory by force of law? If it is compelled by law, what do you authorize the government do to those who peacefully refuse to co-operate or participate?

"Thank you for helping me understand collective responsibility."

She ignored my questions — and reiterated her Big Government proposals.

I apologized for my email failing to reach her — and re-sent her the simple and basic questions above.

That was the last time she wrote.

She's no fool. She has a master's degree. She reads books, magazines, and newspapers. She's been politically active for over 40 years.

Her political words are murky, memorized mantras. She chants the same sacred political sounds that other Massachusetts liberals do. She does not grasp what she believes or why.

Many people have unexamined political beliefs. Unexplored political premises. Untested assumptions.

Very often, our job is not to challenge or criticize the other person's beliefs. We need only ask naive and basic questions. Simple questions.

"I believe that we have a social contract that obligates us to care those who cannot care for themselves," says a politician. Simple questions: 1. What do you mean by the phrase "social contract"? 2. Is this "social contract" like all other legal contracts in America? Is it subject to the same terms, considerations, and limitations? 3. Who is bound by this "social contract" and who is not? 4. Is each person free to choose or refuse to sign the "social contract"? Is it voluntary or mandatory by force of law? 5. If it is compelled by law, what do you authorize the government to do to those who peacefully refuse to co-operate or participate?

"I believe in fair trade, not free trade," says the union official. Simple questions: 1. What do you mean by "fair trade"? 2. What do you mean by "free trade"? 3. How are "fair trade" and "free trade" different? 4. Who decides what's a "fair trade"— the businesses who are trading, or someone not involved in the transaction? 5. Is each person and business free to choose or refuse to trade? Is it voluntary or imposed by force of law? 6. If it is imposed by law, what do you authorize the government to do to those who peacefully act otherwise?

"Because we live in an interdependent world, we need a stronger United Nations," says the world government advocate. Simple questions: 1. What do you mean by the word "interdependent"? 2. Would you give me a few examples of interdependence? 3. What's the opposite of or the alternative to interdependence? 4. Could you give me a few examples of *non*-interdependence? 5. Is each person free to choose or refuse who to have an interdependent relationship with? Is this voluntary or imposed by force of law? 6. If it is imposed by law, what do you authorize the United Nations to do to those who peacefully act otherwise?

Henry David Thoreau urged, "Simplify, simplify."

Henri-Frederic Amiel wrote, "The great artist is the simplifier."

By distilling political ideas to their simple, plain, and basic elements, we can sort the true from the false, the priceless from the worthless.

By asking simple and obvious questions, we can help others to discard meaningless, false, and harmful political beliefs.

How will you know that you are making progress with simple questions?

Easy. Someone will accuse you of trying to over-simplify an extremely complicated political issue.

That's when it's time for you to smile and respond,

"Quite the opposite. You are over-complicating a political issue that we can resolve with a few simple questions. Let's put them on the table — and discuss them one by one. Okay?"

# Watch Your Words

Words can be your masters. Words can be your servants. The wrong words, the wrong phrases can give Big Government politicians and pundits an unfair advantage. The right words, the right phrases will give liberty a free and open intellectual marketplace. That's all we need. Because the facts are friendly to freedom.

How do you determine which words and phrases are appropriate? How do you find the right words?

First, read books and articles by libertarian popularizers. Read libertarian scholars, policy wonks, and researchers for knowledge. But read libertarian popularizers to learn *how* to communicate libertarian ideas and proposals. To learn which words and phrases they use — and how they use them.

Here are a few excellent books by libertarian popularizers: *Why Government Doesn't Work* and *The Great Libertarian Offer* by Harry Browne; *Healing Our World* by Dr. Mary Ruwart; *Atlas Shrugged* by Ayn Rand; *Losing Ground* and *What it Means to be a Libertarian* by Charles Murray; *The Law* and everything else by Frederic Bastiat; *Libertarianism* by David Boaz; and *Libertarianism in One Lesson* by David Bergland.

Second, listen to speeches and training tapes by outstanding libertarian communicators. Listen to what the speakers say — and what they don't say.

Listen to the words and phrases the speaker uses. Listen for modulation and pauses and emphasis. The Advocates for Self-Government has a superb selection of speeches and seminars on tape.

Third, experiment with words and phrases. Pick a libertarian phrase that sounds attractive and try it on a dozen *non*-libertarians. What results do you get? Agreement? Curiosity? Disagreement? Argument?

Let consequences be your teacher. Let results guide your choices in words and phrases.

I regularly test new words and phrases. I keep track of how people respond. I debug. I tweak. I re-design and re-language what I say and how I say it. "Small government is beautiful." was tested. So was "Personal responsibility sets us free."

Here are three test results.

1. President George W. Bush campaigned for an American educational system where "No child gets left behind." The phrasing served him well. People liked it.

Want my tested libertarian re-phrasing?

"'No child gets left behind in our education system.' That sounds good, but here's what it really means: No child will get *ahead* in our education system. Better students will be held back. The best students, the hardest-working students, the smartest students slowed to the pace of the worst students. Do you really want an education system where no child can get ahead?"

2. "Our state government faces a large deficit. How are you going to close the gap on the deficit?"

Tested libertarian re-phrasing: "We don't have a government deficit problem. We have a government *overspending* problem. Legislators are spending more than they're taking in. When are the legislators going to stop *overspending?*"

Talk about overspending, not "deficits."

3. "Our school has a zero tolerance policy with drugs."

Tested libertarian re-phrasing: "Do you know what 'zero tolerance' means? It means 'total intolerance.' '100% intolerance.' A good kid makes a bad choice: total intolerance. A good student makes a mistake: 100% intolerance. No mitigating circumstances. No judgment or discretion. 100% intolerance. Do you really want total intolerance?"

Try out these tested libertarian phrases. Notice the "light bulb look" in the eyes of the people you're talking with.

Try some of your own. Debug them. Tweak them. Re-test the new, improved phrase. And share it with fellow libertarians.

Watch your words. They'll let you reach the hearts and minds of many, many people.

# Try Something Different

"My co-worker is stubborn," said the libertarian activist. "I told him why welfare doesn't work. I told him about *Losing Ground* by Charles Murray. But he just wouldn't budge. What did I do wrong?"

"I've been arguing with my dad about libertarianism for years," said the libertarian student. "It's always the same story. He hates our non-interventionist foreign policy. I've tried Harry Browne's columns. My dad digs his heels in. What am I doing wrong?"

"My best friend fights me tooth and nail over our libertarian position on public schools," said another libertarian. "She's a public school teacher, and she accuses me of condoning ignorance, being against children, and wanting to throw her out of work. Where am I messing up?"

Sound familiar?

Do you sometimes run into a wall when discussing libertarianism with a friend or family member?

From time to time, do you find yourself in fruitless and frustrating libertarian conversations with a co-worker or acquaintance?

Stuck and stalled in dead-end arguments with a neighbor or someone you do business with?

What's wrong with them?

Probably nothing.

What's wrong with you?

Probably nothing.

Then why aren't you persuading them?

I don't know. It may be the wrong issue. The wrong reasons.

The wrong approach. The wrong time. The wrong place. Can you persuade them without knowing what the problem was?

Yes.

If you keep doing what you're doing, you'll keep getting what you're getting.

If what you're doing doesn't work, do something else. Try something different.

A different issue.

If they oppose us on the War on Drugs, talk to them about ending the war on guns.

If they fight you on government-run public schools, talk to them about establishing free market-health care.

If they dig their heels in on immigration, talk to them about the virtues of free trade.

If they won't budge on welfare, talk to them about ending government restrictions on adoption.

If they're against government spending cuts, talk to them about the benefits and blessings of tax cuts.

But what if they oppose you on the new issue?

Pick another issue. Try something different.

Keep trying different things until you find something that works.

What if they're opposed to your approach on issues or politics? Try a different approach.

Consider a non-political example of different approaches. Vegetarianism.

People become vegetarians for many different reasons. Some for religious reasons. Some for moral reasons. Some for health reasons. Some for enjoyment reasons. Some for financial reasons.

If you were trying to persuade a person to become a vegetarian, would you only talk about *your* reasons for being a vegetarian? Or would you try to find out which reasons might most appeal to that person?

There are many paths to libertarianism. Many reasons for becoming a libertarian.

Ethical. Embracing the "Non-Aggression Principle." Opposition to the use of force.

Pragmatic. Freedom works. Freedom is practical and effective and efficient.

Utilitarian. Freedom provides the greatest good for the greatest number.

Egoistic. Freedom benefits you. Freedom is in your self-interest.

Altruistic. Freedom benefits others. Freedom is in their interest.

Outcome. Freedom produces results that you want. It maximizes individual choice. Freedom promotes and rewards personal responsibility. Freedom creates prosperity.

If one road, one reason, or one approach doesn't appeal to the person you're talking to... try a different approach.

If that doesn't work, try another approach.

And when you find a subject or issue or approach that works... keep using it with that person. When what you're doing works, keep doing it.

To make a difference you must do something different.

This is a path to growth and change. For others. For ourselves.

\* \* \*

### If You Always Do
*by Michael Cloud*

If you always do what you've always done,
you'll always get what you've always gotten.
Do you like what you're getting?

If you always do what you've always done,
you'll always feel like you always felt.
Do you like what you're feeling?

If you always do what you've always done,
you'll always be what you've always been.
Do you like what you are?

If you never do what you've never done,
you'll never get what you've never gotten.
Do you like not getting what you're not getting?

# The Moving Parade

You've already talked about libertarianism with your family, friends, and co-workers.

You've told everyone you know about libertarianism.

You've run out of people you feel comfortable talking with.

Maybe you don't want to run for office. Don't want to give speeches.

You probably don't want to talk to strangers.

What can you do to win people to liberty?

Have a brand-new conversation about libertarianism with the people who know you and like you and trust you.

Have a brand-new conversation with people you feel comfortable talking with.

Have a brand-new conversation with your family, friends, and co-workers. With people you socialize with. And do business with. People you're comfortable with.

Am I asking you to impose on, irritate, or offend your family, friends, co-workers, and others you get along with?

Absolutely not!

I'm reminding you of a powerful truth: Things change. Circumstances change. People change.

The last time you talked to Uncle Fred, he'd never had a Close Encounter of the Government Kind. Since then, he got audited by the IRS. And jammed for $13,000 in taxes, interest, and penalties.

Your boss was happily married. Since then, his wife divorced him, got a restraining order, kept him from seeing his children, and he was ordered by the court to pay huge monthly child support and alimony payments.

Your friend Jane had two toddlers. Now her children are school age. And she is so upset with public schools that she is homeschooling her kids.

Your brother felt comfortable with the government. But in the last year, he's gotten familiar with the new "anti-terrorist" legislation — with its invasions of his financial privacy.

Your co-worker is a gun collector. Last year, he was mildly annoyed with "government meddling with the Second Amendment." Since then, many of his fellow gun enthusiasts have recounted horror stories of BATF intrusions, of their local government's revocation of gun licenses, of pediatricians asking their children whether they have guns in their homes. Your co-worker is hotter than a scalded dog about these government violations of his beloved gun freedoms.

A year ago, they were closed to our libertarian ideas.

Today, they are receptive. Ready. Eager to hear about libertarianism. Things change. Circumstances change. People change.

Life refuses to stand still. Life is *not* stationary, static, or frozen forever.

The people you talk to about libertarianism are *not* an audience. They are a moving parade.

They experience small changes and big. Slow changes and fast. Partial and total. Internal and external.

New and different experiences. Changes at home and work. Changes in what they do and feel. Changes in what they know and believe. Changes in the lives of their family, friends, and co-workers.

Those people who were not receptive and ready a year ago — may now be open and eager to hear about libertarianism.

Not all of them. But some of them. Perhaps many.

They are a moving parade.

The people you know and like and trust are changing and developing.

Some toward our libertarian values.

Speak to their new and different and changing lives and circumstances. Share your libertarianism in new and different and changing ways.

Because you have changed and developed.

You are part of the moving parade.

On the way to liberty.

# The Personal Ad Approach

A well-done advertising campaign for a product or service says: "Here are my features, functions, and benefits. Here's what I do for you."

This kind of advertising works. It's tried and true. But it usually costs a lot of money and takes a lot of time.

This approach is effective with marketing liberty, with "selling" libertarianism to new freedom customers.

But there's another very effective way to promote and advance and advertise. It's unconventional. Beautifully individualistic.

The personal ads approach.

Ever read a personal ad?

"Single white female, age 32, seeks single or divorced man, 35 to 45, bright with a sense of humor, established in his career, who enjoys movies, reading, cooking, and cuddling. Children okay. No smokers, heavy drinkers, or drug users, please."

Personal ads do *not* talk about the "product." Personal ads talk about and target a certain kind of customer.

They're designed to attract the kind of customer the advertiser wants. A specific, clearly described kind of person.

They're designed to repel, exclude, and disqualify people who do not fit the preferred customer profile. The low-probability prospect.

Dan Kennedy, an enormously successful marketing wizard, says, "Focus 100% on getting the right people to respond. Simply getting the right people to step forward, raise their hands, and identify themselves to you is enough."

The personal ad has three elements:

1. A brief description of what I'm like.
2. Here's a careful description of the kind of person I'm looking for.
3. If this describes you, if you meet these qualifications, please telephone me at this number, write me at this P.O. box, or email me at this address.

The personal ad lets you talk to only the most likely prospective dates and mates. The high-probability prospects. You can do this with prospective libertarians. Here's how.

Suppose you're talking politics with a new acquaintance. You can use the three elements of the personal ad approach.

1. "I'm a libertarian. As you may know the word 'libertarian' comes from the root word 'liberty.' We advocate individual liberty, personal responsibility, and small government."

2. With questions: "Do you believe that government is way too big?" (Wait for "Yes.") "Do you believe that taxes are way too high?" (Wait for "Yes.") "Do you believe that government is way too involved in businesses, social matters, and our personal lives?" (Wait for "Yes.")

Or with statements: "Libertarians believe that government is way too big, that taxes are way too high, that government is way too nosy, bossy, intrusive, and abusive. We're trying to dramatically shrink the size, authority, and power of government. We're trying to make government small."

3. "Is this what you want?" Or: "If this were possible, would you want it?" Or: "Which parts of this do you agree with and want?"

The personal ad approach is designed to *filter*, not persuade.

The personal ad approach radically reduces the number of debates and arguments. It produces and promotes a greater number of persuasive conversations.

This personal ad approach lets you spend your time with the people most likely to join us. The people most likely to become libertarians.

You'll sign up more people more often as subscribers to the *Liberator Online*. You'll enroll more people more often in the Advocates for Self-Government. Or the Committee for Small Government. Or whatever libertarian groups you support.

Personal ads may bring you love.

The personal ad approach may grow the libertarian movement — and bring us liberty.

# A Second Chance

Have you ever had a promising political conversation go sour?

You coulda, shoulda, woulda opened the other person's mind about libertarianism... except... *this* went wrong or *that* went wrong.

You left something out — or put something in — and things spun out of control.

Have you ever walked away from a conversation like this, muttering to yourself, "If I could do it over, I could have changed his mind?"

If it were possible to have that conversation over, would you want it?

Yes?

Well, you can.

How? By apologizing, asking forgiveness, and asking for another chance.

You are *not* apologizing for something unethical or immoral. You are *not* apologizing for thoughtlessness or bad intentions.

You are apologizing for failing to properly communicate your point. Apologizing for clumsy or ineffective remarks.

If I'm at a party and I accidentally spill a person's drink, I apologize for my blunder, help clean up my mess, and bring them a fresh drink.

If I'm at a party and I accidentally make a mess of a political conversation, I apologize for my blunder, help clean up the miscommunication, and bring them a fresh point, a fresh perspective, a fresh approach.

Here's how to do it.

Imagine that you're in a political conversation. You make a strong point about Big Government social programs. Although the other person seemed receptive, he's now arguing against your point of view. Instead of arguing with him, try this.

1. Apologize. "I'm sorry. That didn't come out the way I wanted." Or: "I apologize. I didn't say that right."
2. Ask forgiveness. "Will you forgive me for messing that up?" Or: "Will you forgive me for saying that so poorly?"
3. Wait until the other person says he forgives you. Until he says, "Sure, no problem." Or: "It's all right. We all make mistakes." Wait until he confirms that he's letting it go.
4. Ask for another chance. "Would you do a favor? Would you wipe the slate clean, and give me another chance to say it right?" Or: "Would you do me a favor? Would you let me start fresh, and share what I really wanted to get across to you?"
5. Wait for the other person's agreement that you have a clean slate, a fresh chance to share your ideas. After he agrees...
6. Present a different point, a different approach, a different insight on the issue that might be more appealing. The point you coulda, shoulda, and woulda made... had you known him just a little better.

You can get a second chance.

In life and in conversations.

Which doubles our chances for a better life... and liberty.

# The Secret of the Persuasion Script File

*Cyrano de Bergerac, Hamlet,* and *The Night Thoreau Spent in Jail* are powerful plays.

Strong themes and characters. Intense drama. Evocative language. Heart-wrenching and explosive monologues and dialogues.

Their powerful scripts cause them to move and touch and inspire us.

How would these plays fare if the actors regularly forgot their lines, stumbled over them, or improvised and embellished them each performance?

"The Gettysburg Address," "Liberty or Death," and "I Have a Dream" are speeches that shake and stir us.

Their powerful scripts persuade listeners to embrace new thoughts, feelings, and actions. They change us.

Imagine them re-written with drab but accurate words and phrases, littered with clichés, re-organized for clarity, and edited for grammar.

"These are times that try men's souls," wrote Thomas Paine. A powerful declarative sentence.

William Strunk Jr. and E.B. White, in their classic *The Elements of Style*, show what it might look like if improvised, edited, or re-written:

- "Times like these try men's souls."
- "How trying it is to live in these times!"
- "These are trying times for men's souls."
- "Soulwise, these are trying times."

Weak. Empty. Ordinary. Forgettable.

The plays and speeches above hold the Secret of the

Persuasion Script File.

Harry Browne uses this secret.

Carla Howell uses this secret.

I use this secret.

You can, too.

A Persuasion Script File is a collection of effective libertarian answers, questions, and phrases.

Suppose you read a libertarian book or essay. Ayn Rand or Harry Browne or Henry Hazlitt. Or hear a libertarian speech. Carla Howell or Charles Murray or Sharon Harris.

You'd learn or discover at least one libertarian answer or question that seems compelling.

So you test it or try it out during a conversation with a non-libertarian. It works. You try it with another non-libertarian. It works again.

If you're scientific and systematic, you'll try several variations of your question or answer, see what results each one produces, and write down the most effective one.

Now you have one tested and reliable Persuasion Script.

Over time, you will discover or learn a number of possible Persuasion Scripts. Every one will need to be tested, re-phrased, and re-tested. Those that work will be recorded in your Persuasion Script File.

You will distill convincing libertarian questions and answers to key social and economic issues. Over time, you will discover, learn, and develop a large and effective Persuasion Script File.

You will have the tools and training to turn people into libertarians. You could have a huge impact on the growth of the libertarian movement. On the achievement of liberty.

Would you like to accomplish a little of this — or a lot?

Because you can start here and now.

Want a fast start for your Persuasion Script File?

    1. Read Harry Browne's *Liberty A-Z: 872 Soundbites for Liberty You Can Use Right Now.* Or Mary Ruwart's *Short Answers to the Tough Questions.* Or read *Liberty and the Great Libertarians* edited by Charles Sprading. Or listen to my "Essence of Political Persuasion" tapes.

    2. Pick a question or statement from one of these

sources — and *test* it on real non-libertarians. Try it on seven to ten different non-libertarians. Do not assume that it has been tested. Do not rely on the other person's experience. Test it yourself.

3. How do you know when your script works? It works when you evoke the response you want from the other person. Does your script open the other person's mind? And perhaps whet his appetite for more libertarian morsels? Does it change his mind?

4. Your script fails when it leaves your listener indifferent or antagonistic.

5. Effective Libertarian Persuasion Scripts work more often, in more circumstances, with more individuals. They are effective, not perfect. They will fail a substantial percentage of the time. As Damon Runyon wrote, "The race is not always to the swift, nor the battle to the strong, but that's the way to bet."

6. Rehearse your Libertarian Persuasion Scripts. Learn them by heart. Make them second nature. This way, you'll always be at your best.

7. Stay hungry. Keep learning and discovering and testing. Keep practicing. Mastery does not come cheap. But it shines.

8. Keep building your Persuasion Script File. Keep working on it.

Harry Browne's extraordinary performances on TV and radio were the result of developing and mastering his own Persuasion Scripts. Of building an exceptional file.

Carla Howell's Persuasion Script File was the foundation of her brilliant performances on TV and radio during her 2002 Libertarian ballot initiative to end the income tax in Massachusetts.

Frankly, this is my secret, too.

You can rise to the heights of libertarian persuasion — if you build a strong foundation with your own Persuasion Script File.

SECTION III

# INSIGHTS & OUTLOOKS

# The Late, Great
# Libertarian Macho Flash

It was a large and expensive home. The architecture radiated impeccable taste. Seated around the dining table were five people: three moderates, a conservative, and a libertarian. The conservative was a multi-millionaire — and a generous political contributor. After dinner she turned to the libertarian and said, "Our hosts tell me you're a libertarian. Maybe I'm a little naive, but I don't know what that word means. Could you tell me about your beliefs?"

"Sure. I can explain them in a sentence: *'F\*\*\* the State!'* Libertarians want to get rid of as much government as they can."

The woman was stunned. She dropped the subject and guided the conversation into other areas. In her mind, two things were associated with "libertarian": bad manners and gutter language.

\*    \*    \*

In the early 1960s, a student asked a spokesman for Objectivism what would happen to the poor in a free society. The spokesman answered, "If you want to help them, you will not be stopped."

What did the student conclude? That Objectivists are indifferent to human need, callous toward the unfortunate, and without solutions to the misery of poverty.

\*    \*    \*

In the early 1970s, on the University of Arizona campus, libertarians set up an information table each week. Armed with the latest books, magazines, and position papers, these libertarians tried to bring their views to the attention of other students. One day a student stopped at the table and asked, "What do you think of Social Security? What kind of help would the elderly get in your free society?"

The student behind the table was an old hand; he had heard the question many times. He responded, "The government has no right to force people to pay Social Security taxes. Taxation is theft. Government has no right to steal from one group of citizens to benefit another. If people don't save money for old age, they have no right to coerce it from those who are working. We should abolish Social Security."

The questioner was shocked. "You want to dump Social Security and abolish taxes? Sure! Maybe we can do without government, too! You don't give a damn about old people. All you care about is your own stinking money!"

This last story is a little painful — I was the libertarian behind the table.

*       *       *

These are three examples of The Late, Great Libertarian Macho Flash.

Most people are familiar with "flashing" — sexual exhibitionism. The common scenario is this: A middle-aged, average-looking man approaches a small group of women or children. He is wearing a raincoat, false trouser legs, and shoes. The man whips open his raincoat to exhibit his naked body. His viewers are shocked, and he leaves before they recover.

The Libertarian Macho Flash has much in common with sexual exhibitionism. A common-looking person exposes his political beliefs in a shocking way. Invariably, he disgusts people or at least shakes them up. The libertarian flasher displays his views in the most offensive way or exhibits whichever views are most likely to offend the audience.

Are some libertarian positions offensive? Not to libertarians. But supporters of other viewpoints may be offended. It depends on the audience. What would enrapture a feminist might offend an educational choice supporter. A liberal might be shocked by a statement that would make a conservative's heart soar. To determine what would flash an audience, a speaker must know who he's talking to and what they believe. He must understand their loves and hates, their hopes and fears. Flashing is emphasizing one's views in terms of what they hate and fear.

There can be many motives for flashing. The flasher is a

show-stopper, a real attention-getter. If someone desperately wants to be noticed, flashing gets instant results. The Libertarian Macho Flash is also a great timesaver. After all, persuasion involves time and effort. By flashing, the speaker bypasses a long and demanding conversation.

Then there are people who live in fear of rejection. Seeing themselves through the eyes of others, they are psychologically dependent, and the possibility of rejection is frightening. How do they handle this? By doing something to get it out of the way as soon as possible. By engineering rejection.

The real macho flasher, by shocking his listeners, convinces himself that his ideas are virile, potent — even intimidating. The audience obviously lacks his intellectual courage and insight. He grasps truth and goodness. He is good, noble, and wise — clearly a superior person. The listeners? They are stupid, worthless, and possibly evil. Why waste time on such inferiors?

Some libertarians flash to convince themselves that they are doing something for freedom. They mistake flamboyance for effectiveness, heat for light.

Still others flash to persuade themselves that nothing can be done for freedom. If people are shocked by libertarianism, then effort is futile. So why try? This is a beautiful example of a self-fulfilling prophecy.

The Late, Great Libertarian Macho Flash has its defenders, of course. They appeal to "honesty," the Lenny Bruce argument, the Ayn Rand argument, or the claim that it works. Each of these falls flat.

The argument from "honesty" goes as follows: It's dishonest to avoid subjects simply because they offend or shock people. As libertarians, we must put moral principles before political consequences. We must fearlessly proclaim our views and let the chips fall where they may.

This won't do. First, if a person implies support for a belief that he doesn't hold, he is deceiving others. But silence need not mean consent.

Second, the purpose of a discussion or speech should determine what one talks about. Suppose an atheist ran for public office. Would a refusal to discuss religion be dishonest? Not necessarily. A speaker isn't obliged to answer every question put to him — only the relevant ones warrant a response. What determines relevance? The nature of the office, the qualifications for holding it, and what the candidate will try to do if elected.

Third, discussing irrelevant issues is misleading. It diverts attention from the real issues and suggests that the irrelevant subjects do matter. This is dishonest.

The Lenny Bruce argument zeroes in on the psychological impact of the Macho Flash. Lenny Bruce believed that frequent use of offensive and shocking words would reduce and ultimately extinguish their ability to evoke strong emotional reactions. If, for example "hell" and "damn" were used often enough, they would lose their power to trigger emotions.

Although true in the long run, this is irrelevant. Twenty years of effort that made America indifferent to libertarian views — rather than violently opposed — would be no victory. It's like running a business deep in the red for 20 years to finally break even. What is the purpose of presenting libertarian ideas: to desensitize listeners to mere words and phrases, or to win agreement on substance? Flashing rarely produces agreement.

Are there any lingering doubts about this argument? Then consider the death of Lenny Bruce. The heroin overdose was incidental — he was hounded to death by those he flashed.

Ayn Rand devised a far more ingenious defense of the Libertarian Macho Flash.

Rand was asked why she used "selfishness" to denote a virtuous quality when it antagonized so many people to whom it meant something quite different. The introduction to *The Virtue of Selfishness* contains her answer. Stated in general terms, it is clear that Rand's attempted justification of her terminology applies to every instance of the Macho Flash.

Rand contended that the popular uses of a given term are no valid index of its correct meaning. A term must not include a built-in moral evaluation, she countered. If a person uses a term in an unconventional manner, perhaps the fault lies with the conventions rather than the speaker. In the name of man and morality, some terms must be saved from conventional abuses. The "exact and purest meaning" of a word should not be surrendered "to man's enemies, nor to the unthinking misconceptions, distortions, prejudices and fears of the ignorant and irrational."

But consider. The meanings of words aren't engraved in stone — they change and evolve. If people don't adapt to changing meanings, they risk being misunderstood. Would Rand care to describe her political views as "liberal" simply because the term would have correctly described them a century ago? No? Then the point is conceded.

Ayn Rand was a virtuoso flasher. Ponder a few of her colorful phrases: "the virtue of selfishness," "capitalism: the unknown ideal," "America's persecuted minority: Big Business," "give a silent 'Thank You' to the nearest, grimiest, sootiest smokestacks you can find," "the evil of self-sacrifice," and "a parasite, moocher or looter."

These phrases are guaranteed to stun the average person. Consider *The Virtue of Selfishness*. If Rand had been interested only in communicating certain ideas, she would have called her book *A Morality of Rational Self-Interest,* or *The Case for Ethical Egoism,* or something equally restrained. But she intended to shock, attract attention, and create controversy. As an author, she could afford to be attacked, but not ignored. Neither apathy nor enemies, however, make for libertarian success.

Contrary to Rand, many terms *do* carry built-in moral judgments. "Treason," "greed," "slander," "stinginess," "kindness," "generosity" and "blasphemy" are but a few examples.

There are, of course, many foolish conventions. But those who regularly flaunt them will pay a price. Far better to use a convention to further one's views!

There are any number of ways to present a viewpoint. The choice words and phrases can dramatically influence whether a position seems beautiful or hideous. A rose by any other name may smell as sweet, but a florist using offensive, ugly names for flowers will soon be out of business. Language can serve libertarian goals or oppose them.

A final alleged advantage of The Late Great Libertarian Macho Flash is this: some people think it's an effective way to persuade others.

This may be true in a limited number of cases.

*Defending the Undefendable* — a textbook case of flashing — may "wake the reader from his dogmatic slumbers" or act like "Drano for clogged minds." But would it be the best introduction to libertarianism? Not a chance!

Flashing should be tested against other methods of marketing libertarianism to the general public. How often does it work? Under which circumstances?

What kind of people does flashing attract?

This is crucial. If the Macho Flash attracts people who will be an embarrassment to the libertarian movement — people who alienate and antagonize, who are crude and ill-mannered — then it ought to be dropped. A political belief is often judged by those who hold it.

And what about the people it does not attract? Will they have open minds in the future, or are they now opponents?

One final point. Some libertarians use the Macho Flash as a litmus test for potential converts. If the listener is alienated by a controversial view, he isn't worth having. Or so these people would have us believe.

This ignores a basic fact of human psychology: changing one's viewpoint usually takes time. Views that many libertarians take for granted today may have seemed ridiculous, insane, or evil in the not-too-distant past. It took many years for even Ayn Rand, Murray Rothbard, John Hospers, Robert Nozick, and Karl Hess to become full-blown libertarians. Thought, study, discussion, persuasion, and time were necessary. And these people are very intelligent. So why does the Macho Flasher expect so much more from a chance listener?

Those who use the libertarian Macho Flash usually discredit libertarianism. People tend to judge a body of beliefs on the basis of a few statements. If a libertarian candidate presents ideas that are virulently offensive to an audience, the audience will assume that his other views are equally obnoxious. In social psychology, this is known as the "halo effect."

Flashing makes enemies. It creates active opponents to liberty. Freedom has enough natural enemies — people who thrive on statism. Why create more through lack of tact?

A viewpoint may be accepted or rejected because of the speaker who presents it. If he is perceived as callous, against all decency, inhumane, and disgusting, then he couldn't possibly be in favor of anything worthwhile. This is a logical fallacy. It is also a psychological fact and not to be ignored.

I have personally field-tested The Late, Great Libertarian Macho Flash. It is not simply unproductive; it is counter-productive. It makes future attempts at persuasion far more difficult. Liberty is the casualty.

What can libertarians do to avoid flashing? I have a few suggestions.

- Know who you are talking to and what they believe. Find out their emotional beltlines and stay above them.
- Before speaking, ask: What are you trying to accomplish? How do you plan to do it? Will your plan promote your goals? Why or why not? Do not stand in the way of your own success.
- If you flash because you enjoy the exhilaration, find other ways of getting kicks. When you do, you will be more emotionally satisfied and politically effective.
- Become politically effective. This will eliminate the desire to prove that nothing can be done.
- Devote your energies to finding more effective ways to bring others to the libertarian philosophy. There are too few persuasive libertarians, and becoming one is a far nobler ambition than seeing how many hearts and minds you can close.

The libertarian movement has matured a great deal. Bright, attractive people are the norm. It is time for our communication methods to come up to date. One step in that direction would be to discard The Late, Great Libertarian Macho Flash.

# You Know Enough About Libertarianism to "Buy" It, But Do You Know Enough to "Sell" It?

"You've answered all my questions about the car, Mr. Cloud," said the woman. "I'll tell my husband what you've told me... and tonight we'll come in and buy the Corolla I picked out."

I was jazzed. My second day out of Toyota's car sales training, and I was finally going to sell a car. Tonight. 1982 was looking good.

I got an early dinner, came back for the evening, and waited. At 8:00 pm, I called my prospect, got an answering machine, left a message, and waited some more.

I finally reached her at 9:30 pm.

"I'm really sorry," she said, "but my husband and I discussed what you said, and we bought a Honda tonight."

Ow! From hero to zero.

What happened? Why didn't they buy the Corolla from me?

An experienced Toyota sales pro took pity on me.

"You should've made an appointment with the lady to bring her husband in tonight, and answered both of their questions. That's probably what the Honda salesman did," he said.

Then he taught me a sales lesson I'll never forget.

"She knew enough to buy the car, but *not* enough to sell it... to someone else: her husband."

In 1970, when I became a libertarian, I knew enough to "buy" libertarianism, but not enough to "sell" it to others.

My questions were answered. My concerns were addressed. My objections were handled. I was sold.

But other people had different questions. Different concerns. Different hesitations and objections.

And I did not know enough about history, economics,

politics, philosophy, religion, or psychology to satisfy them.
I knew enough to "buy," but not enough to "sell."
So I told them why I "bought." I showed them how liberty
answered my questions, met my concerns, and overcame my
objections.
And, if they were the one in 1,000 like me, they bought,
too.
It took a lot of reading, thinking, and talking with fellow
libertarians before I knew enough to "sell" liberty to different
kinds of people.
Maybe you're like I was. Like my friends were. New to
libertarianism.
Maybe you'd like to learn more. So you can better "sell"
liberty.
Would you like to quickly get up to speed?
May I suggest a few books?
*Why Government Doesn't Work* by Harry Browne.
*Liberty A-Z* by Harry Browne.
*Healing Our World* by Dr. Mary Ruwart.
*Libertarianism In One Lesson* by David Bergland.
*What It Means to Be A Libertarian* by Charles Murray
*The Law* by Frederic Bastiat. (A 79-page gem.)
These six books will give you a firm foundation. These six
books will give you enough high-nutrition information to "sell"
to dozens of people you want to win over.
Knowledge and skill will serve you well. And bring more of
your family and friends to a libertarian viewpoint.
The doctor needs to know more than the patient.
The architect must know more than the homeowner.
The cook needs more skills and knowledge than the diner.
You've learned enough about libertarianism to *buy* it. Are
you ready to learn enough about libertarianism to *sell* it?

# Are You an Advocate or a Defender?

"Why are you against public schools? What's the matter with having public schools?"

"If you wouldn't support this gun law, what would you do to make sure we don't have another shooting like Columbine High School?"

"You're against the War on Drugs, but what would you do to keep drugs out of the hands of school kids?"

Are you always on the defensive when you discuss politics and government?

Do you constantly criticize, condemn, and complain about government?

It's an easy trap to fall into. We've all done it.

The solution is simple: Stop defending liberty... start advocating liberty.

What's the difference?

Defending liberty means we are reacting against government proposals or programs.

Defending liberty means we are responding to government actions or policies.

Defending liberty means we are opposing statist ideas.

Defending liberty means they act — and we react.

Defending lets the Big Government crowd set the agenda and determine the rules of engagement.

We must stop thinking like and acting like defenders.

We must think like and act like and *become* advocates.

We must seize the initiative. We must set the agenda.

We must pro-actively determine and define the issues.

We must provide and promote libertarian solutions to

social and economic problems.

We must lead, not follow. We must act, not react. We must make the first move, not passively wait.

We must act first. We must be first to define the problem. We must be first to create and put forth solutions. Libertarian solutions.

We must initiate and support, propose and promote, advocate and advance.

We must be prime movers on issues and problems.

Don't passively wait for the Big Government backers to put forth their solutions. Take the initiative. Define the problem, create a free market, libertarian solution... and call it in to your favorite talk radio *now*. Write it up and email it to your favorite newspaper *now*.

We must demonstrate leadership in the marketplace of ideas. Start the conversation. Begin the discussion. Define the problem, offer the libertarian solution, sketch out three to five benefits that your solution will produce... and ask the others what they like best about your positive proposal.

Make the statists react to our solutions. Let them oppose and criticize. Put them on the defensive.

Take the initiative. Plant the crops of liberty. Don't wait for the weeds of statism.

Take the lead.

Stop defending liberty...

Start advocating liberty.

# The Power of Positive Passion

What do you love about liberty? Not just *like*. Take-your-breath-away, heart-pounding, *love* about liberty? Which dishes on the libertarian menu make your mouth water... turn you on... light up our soul... jazz you... make you want to dance 'til you drop? Which libertarian ideas or proposals turn you on? Stimulate you? Excite you? Make you want to howl at the moon? Which elements of libertarianism make you feel intensely alive? What parts of liberty make you feel like the jazzmen: "Gonna live forever, don't believe in death"?

That passion is your gift. That passion is your strength.

Barbara Goushaw radiates that positive passion when she speaks about "Handguns Are a Girl's Best Friend." Her passion turbocharges her stories and evidence and proofs. She wins the hearts and minds of many skeptics and undecideds... while inspiring freedom's friends.

Marshall Fritz pulsates with high-octane energy when he speaks on behalf of separating school and state. His positive excitement flows through audiences... and readies them for a dramatically different direction for learning and education in America. Because of his positive passion, Marshall Fritz's facts and ideas and options fall on fertile ground.

Richard Rider glows with enthusiasm when he protects San Diego taxpayers against unneeded bond issues, bloated tax hikes, and squanderous government spending. His exuberance and sense of humor, his love of liberty, and his respect for hard-working Americans magnify and multiply his effectiveness. And make his ideas easy on the ears.

Positive passion opens the door... for our libertarian ideas and proposals.

Positive passion wins more converts than irrefutable arguments and unassailable logic.

Positive passion attracts positive libertarians. The best and the brightest. The wisest and the kindest.

Positive passion is remembered long after libertarian information is forgotten.

Positive passion brings people back for more. More passion. More ideas. More information about liberty.

Positive passion is the fuel that drives libertarian principles and information into the receptive recesses of your listener's mind.

Where do you get this positive passion? How do you crank it out?

1. Search your heart for those special libertarian issues that boost your energy, make your skin tingle, stimulate your eagerness and anticipation.

Those are your touchstone issues. Those are the ones that will engage your curiosity. The issues that you will insatiably study and reflect on and talk about.

2. Express your excitement when you speak with others about these issues. Express your excitement *for* our libertarian solutions and alternatives.

Let people see and hear and feel how positively charged you are about our libertarian remedies and recommendations.

Many years ago, a French Impressionist painter appeared at an exhibit of his own paintings. A society matron said, "I've never seen a sunset like that."

"But don't you wish you could?" he responded.

His energy and passion and vision made his art irresistible. As will ours.

3. Stop driving with the brakes on. Stop holding back emotionally. Express your passions. Share you enthusiasms. Celebrate your loves and admirations.

A lot of us need a little help in recovering our emotional expressiveness.

May I suggest a few books that really helped me?

*How I Raised Myself From Failure to Success in Selling* by Frank Bettger. (The first chapter — all seven pages — will show you how to ignite your excitement.)

*Enthusiasm Makes the Difference* by Norman Vincent Peale.
*Zen and the Art of Writing* by Ray Bradbury. (This will awaken your zest — and liberate the passionate speaker and writer in you.)

Positive passion let Richard Cobden and John Bright free England of protectionist laws that were impoverishing working people.

Positive passion gave Patrick Henry the strength to stir the souls of American patriots — and win our independence from Britain.

Positive passion gives you and me hope and belief that liberty is America's destiny.

Positive passion and liberty will triumph.

# The Neglected Art of Listening

*The Quick and Easy Guide to Public Speaking* by Dale Carnegie, *The Sir Winston Method* by James Humes, *How to Write and Give a Speech* by Joan Detz, *Speak Easy* by Sandy Linver, *Speech Can Change Your Life* by Dorothy Sarnoff, and *What's Your Point?* by Bob Boylan.

These are very good books on how to speak.

There are thousands of books on public speaking. Thousands on how to make your point.

But only a handful of books on the neglected art of listening. Why?

Supply and demand. A higher supply of books on public speaking reflects a higher demand for public speaking knowledge and skill. A small supply of books on listening means few people want them.

Most people would rather talk than listen.

People want to be heard. Want to communicate. Want to connect.

Is anyone *really* listening?

Not just remaining silent, but actually *listening*.

Not just half-listening, while watching TV or reading a book or listening to music.

Listening raptly. Listening to what they say and how they say it. Listening to the tones and tempo and emphasis and emotions. Reflecting on the ideas and information. Listening with empathy.

Attentive listening is rare and precious. And desperately desired.

If you practice the neglected art of listening, people will seek you out. They will treasure you.

Why listen?

To learn. To communicate. To connect. To grow.

Would you like to be sought out? Would you like people to tell you what really matters to them and why? Would you like to have people glad that they talked with you?

Here are three keys to high-impact listening:

**1. Home in on phrases and words speakers emphasize — and explore them.** They may repeat or return to them several times.

Naively or gently say, "I notice that you mentioned the word 'equality' several times. Could you explain it to me? Could you tell me more about it?"

Or, "'The social good.' That's an interesting phrase. What do you mean by it?"

**2. Notice what they physically express and emphasize: the phrases and words and ideas and concerns.**

When people express things that are emotionally charged for them, they usually demonstrate it physically. Their voices get louder — or more passionate or more tender. They gesture more. Their faces get animated and expressive.

When they get physically expressive, ask them to tell you more about the concern or idea they emphasized.

Empathize with, "It sounds like that's very important. Tell me about it."

Or, "You're very concerned with this. Please tell me more."

**3. We listen with our eyes. Make warm eye contact with the speaker.**

Open the windows to your soul. He will pour in his virtues and values, his hopes and dreams.

Most people look away from time to time. This helps them process what they're hearing.

But we need to return to friendly eye contact again and again. To let the speaker know that we are paying attention. That we are open to him. That we care.

\*     \*     \*

Do these three things three times during your next conversation and you will be stunned with the results.

The other person will feel understood.

The other person will tell you the things that matter to him.

The other person will reciprocate. He will be receptive to you and your ideas. He will intensely listen to you.

We reap what we sow. We receive what we give.

And it all starts with practicing the neglected art of listening.

# The Other Person's Shoes

"It's called 'In Your Face' libertarianism," said Bob J. "You don't let them get away with any statist garbage. You call them on everything. You hammer them on their coercive, Big Government lies. What do you think of that?"

"You call it 'In Your Face' libertarianism," I responded. "How do *you* feel when someone gets in your face?"

"You're missing the impact of this approach..." he answered.

"We'll come to that in a moment," I said. "But first: how do *you* feel when someone gets in your face? How do *you* feel when someone tries to intimidate you?"

"Well, I guess I wouldn't like it," he offered.

"Close your eyes," I suggested. "Imagine that someone is 'In Your Face.' Shouting at you. Making you feel bad. Like a drill instructor in boot camp. How do you feel? What's going through your mind?"

He opened his eyes. He looked pale. Anxious.

"I couldn't think. I was upset. Nervous," he said.

That's usually how other people feel when someone gets "In Their Face." Afraid. And sometimes angry.

How open to ideas can another person be when he's afraid or hostile?

How well can another person think when he's scared or mad?

To communicate or persuade, we need empathy. To see the world through their eyes. To hear things as they hear them. To feel what they feel.

An old proverb says, "Before you criticize another man, walk a mile in his shoes."

But before we can step into the other person's shoes, we

must take off our own.

Take off our own beliefs. Take off our own knowledge. Take off our own values.

Then try on the other person's. What does he believe? What does he want? What's truly important to him? How does he think about the matter? How does he see, hear, and feel the world?

One empathy error: the "Golden Rule as a blunt instrument" fallacy.

The Golden Rule says, "Do unto others as you would have them do unto you." Some people say, "I would want to be corrected if I said something irrational. I don't mind people raising their voices. I *like* arguments. I wouldn't mind 'In Your Face' libertarianism."

The Golden Rule means: "Do unto others as *they* would have you do unto them." If you were them, how would you like to be treated?

"In Your Face" is a variant of The Late, Great Libertarian Macho Flash, a destructive approach to communication that I wrote about in 1978 (and included in this book on page 119.) Unlike fine wine, this approach grows more toxic with age.

Empathy opens hearts for communication and persuasion.

We don't get it by standing on the other person's toes.

We get it by putting ourselves in the other person's shoes.

# Have You Come Out of the Closet as a Libertarian?

Have you really come out of the closet as a libertarian?

Have you told all of your family, friends, acquaintances, co-workers, and everyone else your life touches that you are a libertarian?

"But you don't understand. My family are all conservatives. And my friends are, too. It wouldn't do any good," one person might say.

"Are you crazy? If I told my family and friends that I'm a libertarian, they'd think I joined some cult like the Moonies," another might offer.

"I don't talk politics, sex, or religion with people. It causes friction. What's the point?" says still another.

Why haven't you told everyone in your life that you're a libertarian?

What are your reasons? What's stopping you from telling? What might happen if you did?

May I show you how and why you will benefit from telling everyone in your life that you are a libertarian?

During the last 20 years, hundreds of thousands of gay men and lesbians have come out of the closet to their families, friends, and co-workers. These gay men and lesbians did it in spite of their fears and fantasies of how people would react.

Some people responded well. Others didn't. A whole lot of people were supportive. Many didn't even care what their sexual orientation was.

Most of these gay men and lesbians experienced a huge sense of relief.

They were free to be who they were.

Hundreds of thousands of people knew the truth. And, since people talk and gossip, so did millions of friends and acquaintances of these people.

Now almost everyone knows someone who is openly gay. And it's difficult to demonize and stigmatize and label people that we know and like and trust.

This is a wonderful example for libertarians.

Imagine family gatherings, parties, and socializing. Imagine coming out to everyone in your life:

"I don't know if you follow politics, but I'm a libertarian. As you may know, the word 'libertarian' comes from the root word 'liberty.' Individual liberty and personal responsibility. That means small government... Small government is a night watchman... a tiny institution... a skeleton crew doing only the bare essentials. That's what I want. I'm a libertarian."

Then ask questions:

"What do you think? Is government too big or too small?"

"Is government too powerful or too weak?"

"Are taxes too low or too high?"

Every time they give you a libertarian-leaning answer, ask them why they believe it. Then ask them to tell you more.

Some of your family and friends and acquaintances will warm to your libertarianism. Others won't. Some will discuss libertarianism. Others won't. Some will agree. Others won't.

But if you and other libertarians follow this advice, millions of Americans will personally know and like and trust someone who is a libertarian.

Millions of Americans will get a positive personal impression of libertarians.

It will be nearly impossible for the media or Big Government politicians to stigmatize and demonize libertarians.

All because you came out of the political closet.

Will you give yourself a gift that keeps on giving?

Will you go to parties and gatherings and work and tell the people in your personal world that you're a libertarian?

Will you come out of the closet as a libertarian?

# The Danger of
# the Big Truth

Adolph Hitler was the master of the Big Lie.

Hitler relentlessly used the Big Lie technique to vilify Jews. He used the "stabbed in the back" Big Lie to explain Germany's defeat in World War I. He used it to promote the Aryan master race myth. He used it to unite Germans against "radicals, defeatists, and pacifists."

Hitler used the Big Lie to lull Europe into a false sense of security. While he prepared to attack.

Why does the Big Lie work?

The size of a Big Lie vests it with credibility. "They couldn't say it if it weren't true."

The nerve of the Big Lie sows the seeds of suspicion. "Maybe it's not totally true, but there must be something to it. Where there's smoke, there's fire."

The Big Lie shifts the burden of proof to those who deny it.

While many people would doubt or reject an implausible small claim, most temporarily suspend disbelief with an outrageous charge.

The Big Lie relied on the fundamental decency of its victims.

It also relied on the difficulty of checking and verifying and communicating the truth.

Before the 1990s, this was pretty easy.

Government-sponsored Big Lies were common in closed societies. It's easy with government-controlled printing, newspapers, radio stations, and television stations.

Now we have the Internet. Web sites. Email. Over 5,000 TV channels available by satellite anywhere on the globe. Hand-cam videos. Cell phones. Faxes. Photocopiers. Instant checking and verifying and responding and communicating.

The Big Lie has a short life today.

Big Lies can be investigated and exposed and discredited and demolished. Hyper-fast.

We are wary about Big Lies. We are resistant.

But that creates a new problem for advocates of reason and liberty.

The problem? The Big Truth.

A truth so big, so extensive, so mind-boggling that many people reject and deny it:

*Big Government doesn't work.* Big Government programs don't work. Big Government programs often make things worse for those they intend to help. Big Government programs create new problems. Big Government programs are wasteful and costly. Big Government programs divert money and energy from productive and positive uses.

When we tell the Big Truth about Big Government, the average person hears this: "Everything you believe about government is wrong."

How would most people react if we told them the Big Truth? Denial, rejection, ridicule.

The Big Truth is too much to swallow.

It is too much to swallow at one sitting.

And that's the key.

We must only offer as much as the person can handle.

Pick one major Big Government program.

For example, show how and why the no-win, insane War on Drugs has dismally failed. How Drug Prohibition has made things worse. How and where it's created new problems — like the early release of murderers, rapists, and child molesters.

Or show how and why our Big Government's war on guns gravely endangers innocent Americans, gives aid and comfort to violent criminals, and shreds the Constitution. Show how and why the 20,000 anti-gun laws on the books have made things worse. Give examples from *More Guns, Less Crime* by John Lott, or the writings of David Kopel, Gary Kleck, Aaron Zelman, and J. Neil Schulman.

Show how and why Big Government means "gun prohibition." And why only libertarian small government respects our right of self-defense and keeps its hands off guns.

Roast and serve one major Big Government program at a time.

Some people need smaller portions. Others want larger helpings. Some people like appetizers. Others want a seven-course meal.

But no one wants to be force-fed.

Few people can digest the Big Truth at one sitting. Persuasion often takes time.

But after they've digested the Big Truth, we may want to offer them a really healthy cuisine:

Small government is beautiful. Small government is simple and cheap and good. Small government is accountable. There's no place to hide waste and corruption in a very small government budget. Small government respects individual liberty and personal responsibility and private property.

# Flat Earth Politics

"We're fair. We present *both* sides of the issue," says the talk show host.

"Unbiased! We let *both* sides present the pros and cons of political proposals," says a TV political talk show.

"Tough and unbiased. We let *both* sides have their say," says another political TV show.

*Hardball. Hannity and Colmes. The O'Reilly Factor. Cross-fire.*

*Full Nelson. Larry King. Face the Nation. Meet the Press.*

They try to be fair.

But they can't.

Why?

Flat earth politics. Flat earth political thinking. Two dimensions.

"Both sides" assumes that there are only *two* sides to an issue. Why not: "All sides"?

"Pro and con" presumes that there are only *two* positions that one can take on a proposal. What if the *wrong* proposal is being discussed? What if the *wrong* question is being asked?

Flat earth politics is the product of the outmoded Left/Right political spectrum.

But flat earth political thinking dominates and controls most political discussions — and talk shows today.

How do we overcome it?

By sharing the World's Smallest Political Quiz with everyone we can. By showing more people that the Quiz's Diamond Chart of politics is more accurate and inclusive.

But there are two powerful things we can add to the mix:

1. Challenge the "two sides" assumption.
2. Add the libertarian alternative.

Consider the issue of homelessness.

Flat earth political discussions would point out the problem of homelessness and then consider only two alternatives... "both" sides:

- The more government alternative. "We need more shelters. We need job training. We need day care. We need treatment facilities." More government programs. New government programs.
- The status quo alternative. "There's a problem, but it's being managed by our present programs. A lot of these people choose alcohol or drugs. Many of them refuse to work." Leave things as they are.

Flat earth politics: More government or leave things as they are.

Where is the "less government" alternative? It's not on the flat earth political map. Not in flat earth political discussions.

How do we overcome this?

1. Challenge the "two sides" assumptions with: "This discussion implies that we have only two basic alternatives: more government programs or leave things the way they are.

"But there's a third alternative: less government. Removing government policies and programs. Would you be willing to consider this alternative... and see whether it would make things better? Would you be willing to *add* a third alternative... so that *all* sides can be considered?"

2. *Add* the libertarian alternative: "What if government programs and policies and powers are causing this problem?

"What if government programs are contributing to the problem... or making it worse?

"What if government programs sustain and fuel the problem?

"What if the solution is not *adding* new government programs, but *subtracting* the programs causing, sustaining, and increasing the problem?

"Let's apply the *third* alternative, the less government alternative, the libertarian alternative to the issue of homelessness.

"First, we need to redefine the issue: the issue is *not* 'homelessness.' The issue is the shortage of cheap and affordable housing and shelter.

"Second, we need to ask which government policies and programs cause or contribute to a scarcity and higher prices for housing.

"Why can Habitat for Humanity build homes for a small fraction of typical building costs? Donated labor and reduced costs of materials is *part* of the answer. But how many government-created obstacles, government-added costs are *not* imposed on our friends with Habitat for Humanity?

"How much red tape is removed? How many needless inspections waived or speeded up? What about other barriers and costs to building? Licensing? Zoning? Endless hearings?

"How much is added to the costs of building homes and apartments by needless zoning hearings, bureaucratic red tape and delays, permits, pointless inspections, mandates, and the like? (Ask people in the construction trades how much this needless government involvement adds to the costs — and the amount of time it takes to build a house.)

"How and where has government blocked affordable housing by zoning and regulating against apartment construction? Or placed barriers and restrictions that push the cost of apartment construction and management so high they're too expensive for the working poor?

"How and where have governments legislated and regulated against mobile home parks? Or temporary trailer parks? How many low-priced homes has this prevented?

"How and where have governments legislated and regulated against multiple-family homes? Where two families could pool their earnings and buy a home that neither family could afford alone?

"The March 2000 issue of *Small Property Owners News* (Massachusetts) has an article on the front page: 'Number 1 cause of homelessness: rooming houses *outlawed*.' How many working poor could *not* afford a house or apartment... but *could* afford a room in a boarding house? How many of these people are on the streets because of government-imposed anti-landlord laws or zoning or regulation or outlawing against these affordable dwellings?

"Forty years ago, Martin Anderson wrote *The Federal Bull-*

*dozer,* a powerful study that documented that the federal government tore down tens of thousands more homes than they built. They demolished 20 or 30 or 40 "sub-standard" homes for every single home they built. So 19 or 29 or 39 poor families were thrown out of their homes — and one got a better home.

"Other studies since then have shown the same pattern: the poorest and weakest are zoned and restricted and bulldozed out of poor housing... and thrown into the street... by the government programs. If you were poor, would you rather have a poor dwelling... or be on the street?

"Which government programs and policies and powers can we remove right now to make housing and rooming more plentiful and cheaper? How many government barriers and burdens can we remove, how many government costs can we eliminate so builders and providers can cut the costs of housing?"

We must consider *all* sides of the issues. We must consider more government, the status quo, and less government.

We must educate flat earth political thinkers — and their audiences.

We must show them the World's Smallest Political Quiz. The Diamond Chart.

We must challenge the "both sides" fallacy and *add* the libertarian dimension. Again and again... until there are at least three sides to every political discussion.

We must become Columbus. And show them a new world. A libertarian world.

# Evangelist or Church Preacher?

"Where liberty is, there is my home," said Ben Franklin. "Where liberty is not, there is mine," reponded Tom Paine. Franklin was the church preacher. Paine, the evangelist.

Some libertarians love to talk with other libertarians about the implications and applications of liberty. They love to flesh out libertarian insights and outlooks. To explore and expand on the finer points of freedom.

Other libertarians love to share their libertarianism with those who have never heard our ideas before. They enjoy introducing people to liberty.

Some libertarian communicators are church preachers. They inspire and elevate our words and deeds. They show us how and why we must be bold and principled. They deepen our thinking and raise our standards. Without them, we might weaken and water down our principles or proposals. Without their influence, we would lose our moral compass.

Other libertarian communicators are evangelists. They get a kick out of talking with people who have never even had a glimmer about liberty. They whet their listeners' appetite for freedom. They find words and phrases and stories and questions that lead their listeners to liberty. Without them, the libertarian movement would stagnate and stand still. Without their steady stream of new converts, we could not grow.

Some libertarians prefer church preaching. Others prefer evangelism.

Most libertarian communicators do one or the other. A handful do both.

Some libertarians believe church preachers are good and

evangelists are bad. Or evangelists are good and church preachers are bad.

We need inward-directed communication. And outward-directed communication. Just as a tree needs roots that reach down — and branches that reach up.

We need to nurture and honor both kinds of communicators. Both are crucial to our success. The evangelist and the church preacher.

# You Are Liberty's Advertisement

*The Boston Globe's* premiere liberal columnist, David Nyhan writes:

"How come just about everyone who ever said to me, 'I'm a Libertarian' seemed bright, well-mannered, at least reasonably dressed...?

"Intelligent, well-informed, articulate, knowledgeable about history and the workings of government, the Libertarians of my acquaintance have been generally upstanding citizens." (April 9, 2000.)

Look at Cato. Observe the Reason Foundation. Consider the Cascade Institute. And Laissez Faire Books.

Look at the Libertarian Party.

And look at the Advocates for Self-Government.

Their spokespeople embody the three C's: Competence, Character, Credibility.

Ralph Waldo Emerson said, "What you are speaks so loudly, I cannot hear a word you say."

But there's Cloud's corollary: "Who you are speaks so proudly, I hear every word you say."

Every time a Cato spokesperson appears on C-SPAN, Fox News Channel, CNN, CNBC, or PBS... he radiates competence, character, and credibility.

Who he is... amplifies his message.

Every time Sharon Harris or Carole Ann Rand or Mary Ruwart speaks on behalf of the Advocates for Self-Government... who she is... magnifies her message.

Who you are dramatically affects what you say. And the impact of your message on the audience.

But it does something more. Who you are substantially influences what people think of our libertarian message. When Sharon Harris gives a speech, she is a living advertisement for the Advocates. She is an advertisement for libertarianism. She is liberty.

When audiences see her — a well-groomed, articulate, informed, and credible spokesperson for liberty — that positively impacts their perception of libertarianism.

When every visible libertarian exudes competence, character, and credibility, this positively shapes public perception of us and our ideas.

But it does something even more important.

Who you are determines who you attract into the libertarian movement.

Like attracts like.

Courteous and civil libertarians like Harry Browne and Charles Murray attract people like them.

Positive and upbeat libertarians like Carole Ann Rand and Marshall Fritz bring people like themselves into the libertarian movement.

Credible and capable libertarians like Dr. Ken Bisson and Paul Schmidt attract people like themselves.

Every one of these new libertarians embodies and radiates the same positive qualities. This creates a virtuous upward spiral.

As we attract more and more individuals of credibility, character, and competence... more and more newspaper columnists, TV personalities, and other public figures will recognize our personal and character virtues.

This increases the chances that libertarianism will get a full and fair hearing.

Every time you dress well and handle yourself well, you powerfully publicize liberty.

Every time you write well and speak well, you advance the cause of liberty.

Because you are liberty's advertisement.

# The Power of Personal Testimony

"How did you come to be a libertarian?" I asked Stacy Van Oast.

"When my baby was born, when I looked into his beautiful eyes, my heart ached with love," she said. "I remembered my public schooling, and I swore that my son would *never* go though that. I knew that I would homeschool him. And that led me to libertarianism..."

Then Stacy Van Oast told me her personal story, her search for liberty. An amazing woman. An amazing story.

"How did you come to be a libertarian?" I asked Carla Howell.

"I was a projects manager in the health care field," she said. "As I examined government rules and regulations and red tape, the government penalties and rewards, the endless and needless micro-managing of health care... as I analyzed and studied the impact of government involvement... I came to realize that government involvement made health care perhaps 10 times as expensive as it needs to be. And that's just the start," she said.

Carla Howell found her way to an Advocates for Self-Government seminar, run by Irwin Jungreis... and then to 24-carat libertarianism. Then she ran as the Libertarian candidate against Ted Kennedy.

Everyone has a different journey to liberty.

Yet every story is powerful and compelling.

Why?

Because the geneticists were wrong. We're not made up of DNA.

We're made up of *stories*. Our lives are woven out of the

stories we live. And these stories engage and involve and change other people's lives.

So many of us are intrigued and involved in the great conversation about liberty... through other people's stories.

Not just facts and logic. Stories.

Personal stories. Personal testimony.

How did *you* come to be a libertarian? Then what happened? Then what? And what did that mean to you?

Share your libertarian story with three *non*-libertarians this week... tell them how individual liberty, personal responsibility, and small government will benefit them and everyone they love... and enroll in receiving the *Liberator Online* or another libertarian email publication.

Stories unlock hearts... and open minds. Sharing stories connects us.

And makes new friends for freedom.

# Articles of Commendation

"How did you become a libertarian?" I asked the speaker at the Washington Libertarian state convention in 1999.

"Brett Wilhelm," he answered.

"What did he say that won you over?" I asked.

"He didn't really say a lot to me. He asked me a few questions, then he gave me an article that made some really good points," he said.

"So the article won you over?" I asked.

"Not the first article," he said. "I came around after I read the fifth or sixth article he sent me. By then, libertarianism made sense to me."

This man was not alone. Brett Wilhelm regularly sends articles of commendation for free markets, property rights, and libertarianism to dozens of people.

Why?

"When I make a case for libertarianism, sometimes people agree and sometimes they disagree," said Brett Welhelm. "Most are uncertain. In the back of their minds is one crucial concern:

"'Sure, you say libertarianism is a good idea. But *who else* says that these ideas make sense, that they're practical? What evidence do you have that you're right?'

"Most of these people won't read a whole book on the subject... not even *Why Government Doesn't Work* or *Libertarianism In One Lesson*. And if they did read it, they might think, 'Well, *one* other person thinks like you do, but I'm not convinced.'

"So I'll find one article from *Reason* magazine on the

subject, photocopy it, and give it to him. Then a week later, I'll give him another article on the subject from Cato. Perhaps another week, I'll give him an article from *The Freeman* or The Heartland Institute. In another week, I'll give him a photocopied chapter from *Free To Choose*. For perhaps six or eight weeks.

"Short and interesting articles. From many different books and magazines. And I try to give him a little less than he wants... so he's hungry for more... and ready to read next week's article.

"If the person doesn't want the articles, he says so, and I honor his request. If he doesn't mind the articles, he is positively exposed to our ideas again and again. If he really catches fire for freedom, I get him involved."

"The secret of business success," said Alexandre Dumas, "is other people's money."

Brett Wilhelm's secret of persuasive success is other people's articles.

Why not clip out articles that make our case for free markets, totally privatizing people's Social Security pensions, ending the insane War on Drugs and Drug Prohibition, and the right to keep and bear arms?

Why not create file folders with six or eight or ten different articles that make the libertarian case on an important issue?

Why not try the Brett Wilhelm approach? Slowly, over six or eight weeks?

Why not pass on articles of commendation?

# Are You Building Libertarian Brand Loyalty?

"When I write letters-to-the-editor, I use the stealth method," said a libertarian acquaintance. "I don't use the word 'libertarian' in the letter. That might alienate some of the readers. I just make the case for cutting taxes, getting rid of this government agency or that, or making government smaller. I let the merits speak for themselves."

"Suppose you convince someone on the issue," I responded. "How will he know that it's a libertarian viewpoint? How will he know that he agrees with a libertarian proposal? And if you don't tell him that it's a libertarian viewpoint, how will he know where to look for *more* sensible solutions?"

If we want free markets, we must *market freedom.*

We must market our libertarianism like Coca-Cola, McDonald's, and Starbucks do.

McDonald's doesn't use stealth advertising. "For a really good hamburger, drive over to 123 North Elm. Bring your family."

McDonald's tantalizes and tempts us. "Come to McDonald's for our mouth-watering, juicy Quarter Pounder... It'll make your tongue dance. Delicious and satisfying. If you're hungry..."

McDonald's makes their brand name convenient and quick. "Right off the 103 exit, with plenty of parking... We know you're hungry. In less than five minutes you'll sink your teeth into your delicious Quarter Pounder..."

McDonald's makes their brand name affordable. "And it's only $1.99 for your lip-smacking Quarter Pounder. Aren't you hungry? Come in to McDonald's for your Quarter Pounder now."

McDonald's advertises "Quarter Pounder," not cheeseburger.

McDonald's advertises "McDonald's," not hamburger stand. Why?

Because McDonald's wants to create and sustain product brand-name recognition and company brand-name recognition.

Because McDonald's is creating and sustaining product brand-name loyalty and company brand-name loyalty.

We don't ask for "cheeseburger." We ask for "Quarter Pounder." We don't go to "the hamburger stand" for lunch. We go to "McDonald's."

Every time they advertise, they remind us to ask for *their* brand, not generic.

When McDonald's provides us with a good meal and a positive experience at one of their restaurants, they *earn* our future business. And we ask for their brand of cheeseburger by name. We talk about "Quarter Pounder" and "McDonald's" by name. Word-of-mouth advertising.

Unless we libertarians brand name our solutions "libertarian," people won't know where to shop.

When you write a letter to the editor, and propose a libertarian solution, proudly label it "libertarian" in the letter.

When you call in to a talk radio show, and offer a libertarian alternative, proudly label it "libertarian."

When you give a speech or have a conversation, and present a libertarian proposal, proudly label it "libertarian."

Some people will begin to notice that every idea they like is libertarian... and they may join us.

Some people will realize that every *real* tax-cut proposal is libertarian... and they may join us.

Some people may find themselves in bookstores and look up and buy libertarian books. Others may seek us out on the Internet.

And as they find that the positions they like, the philosophy they like is *libertarian*, they will develop brand-name loyalty to libertarianism.

The stealth libertarian misses out on all these benefits.

The brand name libertarian enjoys brand loyalty and repeat business.

And he builds a movement and market that will make America a free country again.

# Prospecting For Gold

"Well, I think we need Big Government," the man said to me. "I'm glad we have Social Security and Medicare. While there are some problems, I'm satisfied with public schools. Yes, there are some flaws, but we need welfare. And minimum wage. And the rest of social democracy and our social safety net. I support progressive policies. I think your libertarian society would be huge step backward. What do you say to that?"

"It sounds as though we fundamentally disagree," I said. "Thanks for your time." I smiled, waved goodbye, and moved on.

Why didn't I use my "Art of Libertarian Persuasion" techniques and tools? Why didn't I ask power questions, politically cross-dress our positions, or use persuasive judo?

Why didn't I even *try* to change his mind?

Because I understand gold prospecting.

Prospecting for gold?

Effective libertarian persuasion is like prospecting for gold.

A good prospector needs to know where gold is most likely to be found. The geography, the geology, the indicators, and signs.

A good prospector has to know what gold ore and gold look like. If he doesn't know it when he sees it, he won't know what to throw away and what to keep.

A good prospector needs to know the difference between high-grade ore and low-grade ore. So he can determine whether a vein is worth mining.

Then a good prospector can stake his claim — and use his best techniques and tools to strike it rich.

So, why didn't I even *try* to change the Big Government

supporter's mind?

Because he was either very low-grade gold ore... or had no gold content. And was unprofitable to mine.

He seemed like a nice man. But he was a low-likelihood libertarian.

A smart libertarian prospector concentrates on high-likelihood libertarian ore.

A stubborn libertarian prospector works with everyone equally. Likely and unlikely. Interested and uninterested. Open-minded and closed-minded.

A smart libertarian prospector knows when to abandon a dig and when to cut his losses.

A stubborn libertarian prospector hangs on. He refuses to quit. A smart libertarian prospector keeps mining a rich vein of gold.

A stubborn libertarian prospector keeps mining — even when the vein runs out. A smart prospector enriches himself and his investors. And his gold mine creates capital for those who follow.

A stubborn prospector impoverishes himself and all those who work with him. Many quit prospecting and mining. And believe that striking gold is a matter of luck.

Smart libertarian prospecting means using persuasive tools and techniques when and where and with whom they are most likely to pay off.

How can you tell the difference between high-grade libertarian ore and low-grade libertarian ore?

How can you sort likely libertarians from unlikely libertarians? Ask qualifying questions.

"If it were possible to make government so small it didn't need an income tax, would you want it?"

"If you discovered that Big Government social programs made things worse for the very people they're designed to help — would you be willing to replace them with private, voluntarily funded programs?"

"If you saw that Drug Prohibition and the War on Drugs don't work, make things worse, create new problems, shatter more lives than they save, and are corrupting and wasteful — would you be willing to end them?"

"If you saw that Social Security is a destructive Ponzi

scheme, that it rips off young workers and retirees, if you saw that free-market private pensions and retirement plans are safer and better, would you opt for the free-market, private alternative?"

"If you saw that ending the income tax and leaving the money in the pockets of the people who earned it made more Americans better off more often... would you want it?"

All qualifying questions ask: "If freedom in this area produces dramatically more of what you want for more people... would you want it?"

Qualifying questions let you determine the gold content of the ore. And the freedom potential of the person.

Qualifying questions and smart prospecting will make America free again.

# Teach Liberty
# to Learn Liberty

"Why can't I convince more people to be libertarians?" asked the new libertarian. "I've read *Atlas Shrugged, Why Government Doesn't Work, Restoring the American Dream,* and a whole bunch of other libertarian books, but I don't seem to be getting anywhere with the people I talk to. I get into arguments. I feel frustrated. How did you learn to do it?"

"Give me a moment to think back," I answered.

"How did I learn effective ways to communicate libertarian ideas?" I thought. "Twenty-five years ago, when I was a new libertarian, how did I learn to win people over to liberty?"

I searched my memories for a few moments, then I flashed on the answer:

To learn a subject, teach it. To master a skill, teach it.

To learn libertarian thinking, teach it.

Twenty-five years ago, I would read a libertarian book, say, *Capitalism: The Unknown Ideal* by Ayn Rand.

Then I would *pretend* I was Ayn Rand, use her specific arguments and evidence to present her case, her way on behalf of laissez-faire capitalism.

I would present Ayn Rand's case, step-by-step to someone... and ask whether it made sense to him. And I'd pay close attention to the person's reaction. Positive or negative? What did the person like or dislike? What did the person agree or disagree with?

I would do the same thing, the same way with five or ten people.

I did *not* just tell these people Rand's conclusions. I did *not* just tell the people why Ayn Rand believed this or that.

I treated her arguments like recipes. I copied her pattern of presenting free-market capitalism. Step-by-step.

I taught my listeners exactly how Ayn Rand made her case.

By teaching Ayn Rand's thinking, I learned to think like Ayn Rand. Then I would do the same with Ludwig Von Mises. And Murray Rothbard. And Henry Hazlitt. Frederic Bastiat. Dr. John Hospers.

I would teach von Mises' thinking, von Mises' way. Step-by-step. I would teach his thinking to learn his thinking.

In very short order, I mastered their patterns of thought. I internalized them. I made them part of my skill set. My thought and speech.

By following their recipes, I became a master chef.

Try an experiment. Get a copy of Harry Browne's book *The Great Libertarian Offer*. Read it cover to cover.

Then go to one chapter, say, "How Government Operates" (Chapter 3), and highlight or underline each step of one of Harry Browne's explanations or arguments.

For the next week, tell anyone you talk with, "I just read this really interesting book by Harry Browne. It's called *The Great Libertarian Offer*. Harry Browne said something you might find interesting."

Then present one of Harry Browne's explanations or arguments, step-by-step, as though *you* were Harry Browne.

Ask your listeners what they like best about what Harry Browne stands for. What they most agree with. Which points they found most interesting or thought-provoking.

You become the cook by practicing the recipe.

You learn to present libertarianism like Harry Browne by teaching Harry Browne's words and patterns and points to others.

Would you like to present libertarianism like Harry Browne? Teach Harry Browne's method of presenting libertarianism to others.

You become the dancer by practicing the steps.

Teach good libertarian communication to learn good libertarian communication.

Teach liberty to *learn* liberty.

# Framing Business for the Sins of Big Government

Our United Airlines flight had been sitting on the runway for 40 minutes. Boston's Logan Airport is notorious for delays. The people behind me and in front of me were grumbling.

"I hate these $%©#@! airlines," said the guy behind me.

"They ought to do something about these fat cats," said a man across the aisle.

"The government ought to do something about it," said the woman in front of me.

While pretending to talk to the person next to me, I spoke loud enough to be heard four rows back, and four rows up:

"There must be 10 times as many flights today as there were 22 years ago, before we deregulated the airlines. Probably 10 times as many airplanes in the skies. Free enterprise builds the planes and puts them in the air.

"But Big Government runs the airports. Big Government controls the air traffic. Are there 10 times as many airports as there were 22 years ago, when we deregulated the airlines? Are there 10 times as many gates at the government-run airports? Are there 10 times as many air traffic controllers?

"Government is causing this bottleneck. Free enterprise is generous with airplanes, but government is stingy with airports, gates, and air traffic controllers.

"Then government frames and blames the airlines. Government tells us it's United's fault. Or Delta's. Or American Airlines.' The airlines have solved their part of the problem: getting us planes and getting us seats. But government can't deliver the airports, the gates, or the air traffic controllers needed to fly us safely and on time. We're stuck on this runway because of government-created scarcity.

"What do you think?" I asked the person I pretended to be talking to privately... while making a statement to the people around me.

"Gee, I've never really thought about it," he said. "But you know, the government hasn't made Logan Airport much bigger in the last 20 years. It's kind of like the Big Dig, isn't it?" (The Big Dig is a typical government highway project in Boston: way over budget, late, and a mess.)

The people in the seats in front of and behind me started discussing who caused the delays in our flight. These Massachusetts flyers openly discussed how much government was at fault.

Here's how Big Government frames business:

First, government loudly accuses business of causing the problems created by government. Then they blame business and free enterprise for the costs and consequences of the problem.

For example, government blames responsible gun manufacturers for gun crimes. Then government blames responsible gun owners for the violence caused by the Drug War.

Gun violence has doubled since the War on Drugs. Need another example? Compare gun violence during alcohol Prohibition to gun violence before and after Prohibition.

Government frames and blames HMOs for high health care costs. But the government created HMOs in 1974 and mandated their use in the early 1980s. Further, government spends 52 cents out of every health care dollar in America and regulates 100% of all health care services. Health care is the most government-regulated industry in America.

Yet in 1999, the Amherst, Massachusetts town government passed a resolution to "end the free-market carnage in health care." And the U.S. Congress regularly subpoenas and interrogates health care providers in front of television cameras... blaming HMOs for the crimes of government.

Libertarians need to think through and explain the following:

- How does government increase the cost of the business you're discussing?
- How does government regulation create scarcity and reduce consumer choice?
- How does government red tape drive small busi-

nesses out of business?

- How does government increase the cost of everything you buy? Taxes, restrictions, zoning, unfunded mandates... and what else?
- How does government slow down service and reduce staffing?
- How does government cause or contribute to the very problems they blame business for?

To be effective, we must be well-informed. We need to read books like *The Great Libertarian Offer* and *Why Government Doesn't Work* by Harry Browne; *Freedom in Chains* and *The Fair Trade Fraud* by James Bovard; *Losing Ground* and *What it Means to be Libertarian* by Charles Murray.

As Thomas Huxley said, "A beautiful theory, slain by a gang of facts." The facts are friendly to freedom.

Sometimes no persuasion is necessary. We merely need to inform and educate. To show how, where and why government has caused certain problems, or made them worse.

Sometimes all you need is a captive audience, a voice that carries, and a few thought-provoking facts and explanations.

# Save Your Breath

Mr. J said, "Your idea about privatizing Social Security intrigues me. But I'm really unsure about the numbers. How much could we realize from the sale of federal assets? Could we really be sure that everybody saved for their golden years? And what if they didn't? What about these people?"

Ms. R asked, "But if we did end the War on Drugs, could we really be sure that a lot of kids wouldn't go out and get hooked? If people are buying drugs while they're illegal, wouldn't more people buy them when they're legal? Can you show me that it would work out as well as you think it would?"

Mr. D said, "Your idea about making the federal government so small it doesn't need an income tax is really interesting. But how would we handle welfare? What about people that bought assault weapons or machine guns? And if the FDA didn't handle impartial testing of pharmaceutical drugs, wouldn't we get a lot of shoddy and substandard drugs and wouldn't people die? And if what if the Department of Agriculture didn't inspect beef or milk?"

You've probably heard questions like these many times. I have.

You probably spent a lot of time explaining how and why the marketplace would meet these needs and provide better service at lower cost.

You probably explained how the voluntary way is generous and effective.

Sometimes you had great discussions. Sometimes you realized you needed to study up on the subject a little more.

But many times you found yourself embroiled in endless

arguments and debates.

"After all, didn't the Industrial Revolution give us sweat-shops, robber barons and child labor?"

"And before Medicare and Medicaid weren't there millions of Americans who went without medical care?"

"And what about those greedy corporations polluting everything in sight?"

"And lumber industries clear-cutting everything beautiful and leaving Bambi with no place to live?"

And at the end of a two-hour, knock-down, drag-out debate, with every anti-free-market cliché, every anti-capitalism myth taught in our government-run public schools and colleges... you probably needed a cold glass of milk, a cookie, and a nap.

That's the way I used to feel at the end of those kinds of debates.

That's when I learned the "Save Your Breath" technique.

When someone raises objections, when they want to know what the numbers are, or all the details about the plan, or more history than you ever learned in school... you need to save your breath.

Whenever they want to see your plan, when they ask for complete details, when they want to go through the complete history of American business, when they want to know what your numbers look like... save your breath.

How? Ask them:

- "If the numbers are right, do you want it?"
- "If the plan is workable, do you like the concept?"
- "Suppose history bears me out. What will you do?"
- "If the facts show us, if the numbers show us that this approach is dramatically better than what we have today, will you support it?"
- "Suppose I'm right. Do you like the approach?"

Before you go into proving your case, before you go into selling the product, make sure they want it.

Before you sell the details, before you sell the "How," ask if they like the approach.

Ask if they like the concept. Ask if they like the premise.

If they answer, "No," the discussion's over. It doesn't matter. It will have zero impact on their beliefs or behavior. There's no reason to bother.

Save your breath.

If they say, "I'm not sure, but I'm interested," (which is what many people say when they don't want to commit), ask them, "Are you interested enough to read just one book cover-to-cover on the subject?" "Are you interested enough to spend a couple of hours of your time to take a thorough look at the facts?" Usually, the answer is "no." If so, save your breath.

But if the answer is "yes," ask them to read *Why Government Doesn't Work* or *The Great Libertarian Offer* by Harry Browne. Or *The Incredible Bread Machine* by Richard Grant. Or *Libertarianism* by David Boaz. And be sure to sign them up for the *Liberator Online*, so they can read Dr. Mary Ruwart's "Short Answers to the Tough Questions" column.

If they answer, "Yes, I like the approach." "Yes, I like the concept," tell them some of the details. Give them some of the facts that you've learned. But then ask them if they would do you a favor. Would they be willing to take just a little bit of time and read a really important book that could answer all their questions? And then give them their choice of any of the above books.

If you talk to the same kind of people I do, about 50% would say, "No it wouldn't make any difference."

Thirty to 35% will be "interested," and a small fraction of them will be interested enough to learn more.

And the remaining 15% will say yes.

Save your breath on the no's. Save your breath on the "looky-loos" who are "just interested." But cherish, educate, and communicate with everyone who says yes. These are the people you saved your breath for.

# High-Impact Libertarianism

"I explain our libertarian positions to people, and they seem to agree with me... but their eyes don't light up. Their pulse doesn't quicken. They don't get nearly as excited as people who *really* get turned on by libertarianism," said Mr. G.

"People agree with me, but they don't get involved. They don't sign up with the Advocates, or enroll in the Libertarian Party, or start buying from Laissez Faire Books," said Ms. L. "Why aren't they joining?"

"All my friends are libertarians now," said Mr. Q. "But they don't help, don't donate, don't join, and don't vote. Why not?"

They don't see the huge difference that libertarian changes could make in their lives.

They do agree with us. But it's just not that important to them. Yet.

They've seen the light, but they haven't felt the heat.

They don't want liberty bad enough.

Why not?

We have explained what libertarianism is. How it works. Why it's good and right.

But we've left out one vital ingredient.

Motivation. High-impact motivation.

We must show the huge, immediate, direct benefits of liberty to them, and the people they care about.

Huge, immediate, direct benefits. That's the key to motivating them to act.

To believe in liberty is not enough. We must act for liberty.

To persuade people to act for liberty, they must expect huge, immediate, direct benefits.

Every libertarian principle and policy has consequences. When we're discussing a libertarian policy or proposal, we must clearly and compellingly show the consequences that would have a high impact on our listener's life.

We must connect the consequences to our listener.

Imagine the huge, immediate, direct impact of ending the income tax.

Imagine the huge, immediate, direct impact of releasing young people from the prison of the Social Security system.

Imagine the huge, immediate, direct impact of ending the no-win, morally wrong War on Drugs.

For example, what would be the financial impact of ending the income tax to your listener?

1. He'd get to keep all the money he earned. To save or spend or give away as he saw fit.
2. So would everybody he knows and loves.
3. Everyone who does business with him would have more money to spend with him.
4. So would everyone else.
5. Government would not have this money. They couldn't fund their ineffective, harmful programs. Nor put their burdens on taxpayers' backs.

What would be the sixth positive high-impact consequence? The seventh? The eighth?

Every action has multiple consequences. Every consequence has consequences.

As Frederic Bastiat observed in his famous essay, "What is Seen and What is Not Seen," we must trace out the extended consequences of each choice and action.

High-impact libertarianism requires us to vividly communicate the huge, immediate, direct impact of our policies to our listeners.

What's in it for them?

What's in it for the people they care about?

What are the biggest, best, fastest, most direct benefits that this libertarian change will give them?

How will their lives be dramatically different? Substantially better?

Are you using high-impact libertarian communication?

The test is really simple. Are they signing up? Are they

enrolling? Are they joining? Are they donating money or time? When we make it matter to them, when we make it urgent to them, we move them to action.

High impact means involvement, not just agreement.

High impact means their behavior changes.

High impact means action.

# More Rational Than Thou?

"I have an interesting story for you, Michael," said Mr. R.

Mr. R has been a libertarian for over 25 years. His stories are always interesting and often instructive.

"A lesser-known libertarian wrote an essay against the War on Drugs. I thought he put together a pretty good argument," said Mr. R. "So I asked one of my relatives to read it. She was conflicted by the facts and arguments that the libertarian writer presented. But she was willing to be challenged.

"Until she came across one sentence in the middle of the essay..." sighed Mr. R.

He had my attention. "What was that one sentence?" I asked.

"The libertarian writer said that 'Only libertarians are logical.' My relative threw the essay down, and said 'That's insulting.' That libertarian writer alienated one person who was willing to consider our proposals regarding the War on Drugs," said Mr. R.

Are libertarians the only logical people?

Are libertarians the only people guided by logic, reason, and the evidence?

I've been in the libertarian movement for over 30 years. I've met rational libertarians, and those who fall short. I've met logical libertarians, and those who may have misplaced a syllogism or two.

Libertarians are as diverse as any other group. We find the best, the worst, and everyone in between.

The question is not: Are all libertarians always logical?

Nor is the question: Are only libertarians logical?

Nor even: Do the arguments and evidence support the libertarian position on ending Drug Prohibition?

The interesting question is this: How do you feel when someone who disagrees with you claims that you are illogical?

How do you feel when someone claims to be... more rational than thou?

How do you feel when someone labels you as defective or flawed?

I feel defensive. Maybe combative. Insulted. Put down.

Probably you do, too.

When I'm slammed or damned, I find it hard to keep an open mind. Unable to risk new and unfamiliar ideas.

"Only libertarians are logical" means: If you disagree with me, you're illogical.

"Don't blame me... I voted Libertarian" means: I blame you, because you didn't.

"Libertarians are more rational" demonstrates conceit. Arrogance. Smugness.

This attitude closes other people's minds.

It shuts down communication. It hurts and angers.

Self-righteousness loses friends and alienates people.

To persuade, we must respect the other person. We must put ourselves in the other person's shoes.

Persuasion realizes that no group and no philosophy owns the exclusive rights to logic and rationality.

Persuasion reaches out with an open hand, not a clenched fist.

Persuasion is a gentle art. It recognizes that we are human, all too human.

Persuasion says, "As human as thou."

# Take Out the Trash

"Every time I talk to my brother about libertarianism, I get frustrated," said Mr. J. "When he doesn't understand or agree with me, I get really curt. Sometimes I shout like a drill instructor. I practice the communication skills I learned from the Advocates and your 'Essence of Political Persuasion' tapes. How come I'm not using these skills?"

"Sometimes I feel like shaking people until they pay attention," said Mr. N. "I tell them what I've read in Harry Browne's *Why Government Doesn't Work*, but it just rolls off them, like water off a duck. Then I repeat it, because I figure they didn't get it. What's going on?"

"With most people, I communicate libertarian ideas really well," said Ms. D. "But when I tell my family about libertarianism, I just lose it. I'm like a 9-year-old girl, bickering with my brothers and sisters. Why am I acting this way?"

Why do smart, well-educated, concerned communicators mess up like this?

Because they're not taking out the trash.

Trash?

Communication patterns that don't work. Communication habits that make things worse. Toxic attitudes. Harmful emotional triggers.

For example, you may know that yelling at your son doesn't work. He doesn't do what you want. So what do you do? Yell louder. Yell longer. Yell repeatedly. And finally, because you're bigger, he loses. Is that what you really wanted?

These toxic communication patterns occur between parents and children, brothers and sisters, friends, people we socialize with, co-workers, and others.

Why do we resort to communication patterns that don't work? That make things worse?

We forgot to take out the trash.

Trash techniques of communication emerge when we are hungry, angry, lonely, and tired. When we're frustrated. When we're at our emotional worst.

What kind of trash techniques?

1. Chinese water torture techniques, where we drip, drip, drip the same points, in the same way, on the same people. Repeated debates with the same people. Endless arguments over the same issue with the same people.

2. Toxic emotional expressions. Anger. Frustration. Pain. Fear. A voice cold as ice. Expressions that make us defensive or antagonistic.

3. Personal favorites. Everyone has communication methods that don't work. That make things worse.

Most of us know our own Achilles' heels. If not, our friends will be happy to enlighten us.

For example, when I feel frustrated, I become very abrasive. Sandpaper on sensitive souls. Sometimes I shout. This doesn't work and it makes things worse. And I do it anyway. Because I have my own personal flaws, just like you do.

Fortunately, my friends are not shy about helping me grow spiritually. So I know what belongs on my personal trash list. And I do my best to take out my own trash.

These trash techniques keep us from reaching the hearts and minds of people we care for. They block us. They hold us back. They sabotage us.

We need to take out the trash.

We need to remove these techniques from our bag of communication choices.

Would you like to take out the trash?

Make a list of how you communicate when you're frustrated. Of how you communicate when you're angry. Or hurt.

Search your memories for discussions where you blew it. Where you did stuff that didn't work. That made things worse. Where you frustrated other people. Made them angry. Freaked them out. Write these down.

Talk to your family and friends. Ask them what your communication flaws are. What you do that really bugs them. Tell them that you're trying to clean up your communication. Write these down, too.

If you're like most of us, you have between three and seven Basic Trash Techniques.

Take a sheet of paper. Draw a horizontal line near the top. And draw a vertical line from the top to the bottom.

On the left side of the paper, list each of your Basic Trash Techniques.

Now we need to brainstorm what you're going to do instead.

If you only empty the trash, the next time you get into a frustrating discussion... you'll carry the trash back in.

Vince Lombardi said, "Fatigue makes cowards of us all." True. But frustration makes fools of us. And we carry the trash back in. Human nature.

We must replace trash with treasure.

It's not enough to resolve, "I'll never do that trash again." Remember, the road to hell is paved with good intentions. The road to heaven is paved with good habits. So we must find treasure techniques to replace our trash techniques.

What will you do instead? What will you replace the trash with? What will you substitute for the techniques that don't work, that make things worse?

Brainstorm out three positive patterns you can substitute for each trash technique. Ask your friends to help you. Re-listen to the "Essence of Political Persuasion" tapes. Go to back issues of the *Liberator Online* for "Persuasion Power Points" (at www.TheAdvocates.org). Re-read *How to Win Friends and Influence People* by Dale Carnegie. Or *Winning Without Intimidation* by Bob Burg.

On the right side of that vertical line, directly across from each trash technique, list several treasure techniques.

A good rule of thumb: three treasure techniques for each trash technique.

Why three? Because one of the treasures might be high-gloss trash. You'll never know until you try it. And after you discover it's high-gloss trash, you'll want to substitute one of your other two treasures.

Practice each treasure technique in front of a mirror. Ten

times. Every time you take out the trash.

The road to heaven is paved with good habits. Practice makes permanent.

In our home, we take out the trash once a week. The garbage man picks it up, and hauls it away.

With communication habits, you may want to take out the trash once a day. It only takes 10 minutes.

Then, as you clean up your communication, you might want to take out the trash once a week.

Then, once a month. But no matter how good you get, you'll always need to take out the trash.

# Optimism Pays

Why do some libertarian activists persist and persevere? Why do others simply give up and quit?

Why do some libertarians spotlight and lead cheers for libertarian progress and success?

And why do some others heckle other activists, throw verbal brickbats, and serve as boo-leaders against our fellow libertarians?

Why are some libertarians optimists while others are pessimists? And what difference does it make in their libertarian activism?

### Why pessimism?

Watch local TV news. Seventy-one percent of the content is negative and helplessness-invoking.

Death. Destruction. Depravity. Despair. Depression. And there is nothing the TV viewer can do about most of it.

Gossip is mostly negative.

"Isn't it awful about Mary?" Then the person gives gruesome details about how rotten things are for poor Mary.

"Have you heard what happened to Steve?" The news of his firing, gambling problem, drugs, alcohol, snotty kids, rotten relatives, or nasty neighbors is just too juicy to keep to yourself.

Toxic talk gets shared and passed on.

Add a bad work day or a bad experience with someone in your life, and the news and gossip seems even worse.

Bad news triggers bad memories. And creates a vicious downward spiral into pessimism.

A pessimistic attitude triggers inertia or unhealthy behavior. Bickering with your loved ones. Overeating or drinking too much. Goofing off. Spending time in unsatisfying ways. Pessimism costs.

Now imagine that the pessimist is a libertarian. He'll pass on bad news and toxic gossip about fellow libertarians. He'll find fault with everything and everyone libertarian. He'll criticize and complain and condemn.

Non-libertarians who know him will judge the rest of us based on his attitudes and actions.

He'll repel productive libertarians. He'll undermine active libertarians. He'll weaken our efforts.

## Why optimism?

Optimism pays. A growing body of evidence shows that optimism pays off in many spheres of human activity.

Optimists live longer than pessimists.

Optimists have fewer illnesses and diseases.

Optimists recover from illnesses and diseases more quickly and more often.

Optimists are happier and experience more positive moods. Why?

They socialize more often. When people socialize, 82% of the time they report better moods.

They are more physically active. And they take better care of their health.

Optimists are more successful in work, in the arts, in sports.

In *Learned Optimism*, Martin Seligman cites example after example of optimists' career successes.

Optimistic real estate agents sell 250%-320% more than pessimists. Optimistic insurance sales people outsell the pessimists by 88%. Pessimists are three times more likely to quit than optimists.

Why?

Optimism produces persistence. In the face of setbacks, optimists persevere.

Pessimists give up.

In sports and the performing arts, the optimists practice 33% to 50% more than average competitors. In academics, optimists will study 40% more than average students.

Because they expect their efforts to pay off, optimists work longer and harder. Because they work longer and harder, they reap what social scientists call "cumulative advantage." Increasing returns. Optimists are able to delay gratification. Because they know that perseverance pays. Optimists view setbacks as temporary, limited, and surmountable. Optimists bounce back from life's blows. Optimists are able to capitalize on good events. Because they believe they can make things even better.

The libertarian optimist can deal with "slings and arrows" of fate.

If a libertarian political campaign does less than hoped, the optimist learns from his errors and finds ways to make the next one better. The pessimist shoots the survivors.

If a libertarian outreach project fares poorly, the optimist asks those involved what worked and what didn't. Together they plan their next outreach effort. The pessimist says, "I told you so," and "It's no use."

The libertarian optimist turns obstacles into opportunities. The libertarian optimist turns opportunities into huge payoffs.

His optimistic words and deeds attract positive and productive libertarians. Strengthens and energizes them.

He has setbacks. He makes mistakes. But he recovers and moves on.

He builds on progress. And because like attracts like, he draws in others like him. He attracts the lights of liberty.

### Can you learn to be an optimist?

Yes. You can learn how to think, speak and act in ways that make you more optimistic.

In *Learned Optimism*, Martin Seligman shows how and why a person's "explanatory style" powerfully impacts on our moods and behaviors.

Why a pessimistic explanatory style treats setbacks and defeats as permanent, pervasive, and personal. How it depresses us and makes us give up.

He shows why an optimistic explanatory style lets us treat obstacles and hardships as temporary, specific, and external.

He shows us how to become an optimist by thinking and

talking like an optimist.

In *Feeling Good*, David Burns provides us with the tools and techniques to deal with life more effectively and positively. *Adversity Quotient*, by Paul Stoltz, teaches us the patterns of active optimism.

There is no utopia. There is no heaven on earth. None of these books promise a problem-free life.

But they give you the tools and training to enable you to do far better, far more often.

And to feel more upbeat and enthusiastic while you're doing it. At work. At home. When you socialize. In your libertarian activism.

Pessimism costs.

Optimism pays. Politically and personally. Now and in the years to come.

Optimism persuades. Optimism pays.

                                *       *       *

Suggested reading:

*Learned Optimism* by Martin E.P. Seligman, Ph.D. (The best book for transforming yourself into a tough-minded optimist.)

*Adversity Quotient* by Paul G. Stoltz, Ph.D. (Highly recommended.)

*Positive Illusions* by Shelley E. Taylor

*The Power of Optimism* by Alan Loy McGinnis

*Feeling Good* by David Burns

# Politics Is Personal

Watch the talking head political shows on TV.

Notice that politics is general, not specific. Impersonal, not personal.

Conventional attitudes. Only two points of view. General answers.

Liberalism. Conservatism. Middle-of-the-road.

*Hannity & Colmes. Tim Russert. The O'Reilly Factor. Hardball with Chris Matthews. Larry King. Charlie Rose.*

These shows debate issues from on high. Like philosopher kings.

Should we do this or should we do that?

Should we raise this group's taxes or that group's?

Should we pass this new law or that new law? Or should we be reasonable and compromise... and pass both laws?

If you watch enough talking head shows, you'll notice something very interesting.

Each side vilifies the other. Each side claims to be on the side of angels. Each side promises that its proposal will benefit America.

But the promised benefits are vague and general.

Then each side promises benefits to a specific class of Americans. Union members. Women. Teachers. The elderly. Or... the children.

What's missing? Specific consequences. Concrete benefits. Immediate payoffs. Direct advantages.

This is a huge opportunity for libertarian communicators.

We must fill in the blank.

We must make politics personal.

Freedom is personal. Responsibility is personal. And so are
the consequences of every government policy and program.

We must reclaim the political discussion from the talking
heads and philosopher kings.

We must discuss the personal impact of politics.

How?

Politics is not an abstract issue. The War on Drugs. Gun
control. Taxes. Minimum wage. Social Security.

Politics is personal. Economics is personal. Because they
directly impact on you, your neighbors, and everyone you care
about.

Libertarians must show how and why a government program or policy impacts on each of us.

To do this, we must trace the consequences of the law. And
the consequences of the consequences.

A pebble in a pond creates multiple ripples. Multiple waves.

And so does every government program and policy.

Detective novels tell us to "follow the money."

Libertarian thinking tells us to "follow the consequences."

Stop talking about abstract politics. Start talking about the
policy's consequences. Then, "follow the consequences." From
Washington, D.C. to your community. To your family and
friends.

Identify the impact of the government policy or program to
you and your loved ones.

What other consequences does it create?

Do these consequences make you better off or worse off?

Do they save you money or cost you money?

Do they protect you or threaten you?

Suppose the federal government raises the minimum wage
to $8 an hour.

One talking head will say we need it to guarantee a livable
wage for the poorest Americans.

The other talking head will say that $8 an hour will impose
a burden on business, or increase black teenage unemployment, or be bad for America. (Thomas Sowell and Walter
Williams would surely agree. As would I.)

But this fails to personalize the issue. And politics is
personal.

We must ask, "What would be the consequences of raising

minimum wage to $8 an hour?"

What would be the impact on small business? What about employees? Employers? Customers? Investors? What are the immediate consequences? What are the secondary consequences? Follow the ripple all the way across the economic pond.

Eight-dollars-an-hour minimum wage. (Plus all the other government-mandated "benefits" that a business must pay for.) A short-handed local business was hoping to hire one more employee. Now they can't afford him.

So he has no job. Instead of starting for $6 an hour, instead of developing job skills and getting experience, he's priced out of the job market.

He may turn to welfare. To food stamps. To housing vouchers.

And you and I are paying taxes to support this person who has been forced off the job market by the minimum wage.

What about the owner of the small business? He has to put in extra hours to make up for the employee he cannot afford to hire. So he works an additional 10 hours each week. For no extra pay. Away from his family and friends.

But it doesn't end there.

Trace the consequences. And the consequences of the consequences.

You're a customer of the store. When you shop there, you can't find an employee to help you find the product you're looking for.

So your shopping takes you ten minutes longer. And because they can't afford an extra check-out clerk, you spend an extra five minutes in line.

Minimum wage didn't simply cost a young man or woman their job, it also cost you 15 minutes of your life. And it cost every other customer in the store 15 minutes of their lives.

Not once, but every time you shop there.

This is one simple example of tracing the consequences.

Politics is personal.

It is not enough to say, "This is wrong because it interferes with the market process."

Or, "This is wrong because it coerces people."

We have to trace the rippling consequences of the policy.

Politics is personal.

We must sketch out the negative consequences of government policies.

And the positive consequences of individual liberty, personal responsibility, and small government.

Liberty is personal. Prosperity is personal. A thriving economy is personal. Good work is personal.

Low prices and prompt service are personal. Every time you shop.

Life is personal.

We must personalize politics.

When people see the blessings and benefits of liberty, they have a personal stake in supporting libertarian proposals, candidates, and policies.

Make liberty personal. You'll reach the hearts and minds of those who matter to you.

# The Toughest Prospects: Family and Friends

"I don't know why my dad supports single-payer health care," said my friend. "He's smart. Well-educated. He was a business leader. He understands most of our libertarian philosophy. But he insists that single-payer health care is the only solution to our health-care problems. What can I do to change his mind?"

"How many times have you discussed health-care policy with your father?" I asked.

"Several times," she said.

"How many libertarian policy proposals, white papers, articles, and books on the subject have you asked your father to read?" I asked.

"Maybe 10 or 20 articles and books," she answered.

"When did you start trying to convince your father about free-market health care?" I asked.

"Four or five years ago," she said.

"Is he any closer to agreement than he was when you started?" I asked.

"No, he hasn't budged an inch," she admitted.

"Since he's not buying, why are you trying to sell?" I asked.

"He's my dad. He's seen the evidence. He ought to agree," she said.

"But he doesn't agree. He's no closer to agreeing. He doesn't want to agree. And, much as you love your father, he may never agree. If he never agrees, if he never becomes a libertarian, will you still love him?" I asked.

"Of course. I love my father. I'll keep loving my father whether we agree or disagree," she said.

"May I make a suggestion? Accept that your dad doesn't see health care the way you do, that he doesn't want to change his mind, that he probably will never change his mind. Drop the health-care issue. And cherish the relationship you have with him," I said.

Often, the toughest prospects for liberty are our family and friends.

If you've given your family and friends books and articles about libertarianism, if you've have many discussions and arguments with them, and if they are no closer to libertarianism... drop the subject.

If they're resisting, stop pushing.

If they're not buying, stop selling.

Maybe they don't like the ideas. Maybe you're pressuring them. Maybe you are the wrong person to convince them.

Relax. Savor the moment. Enjoy your relationships.

Stop demanding that family or friends absolutely must agree with you.

Talk to people who are interested in libertarian ideas and solutions. Talk to high-probability prospects.

Maybe someday your family and friends will come to libertarianism. Maybe they won't.

Accept them as they are. Love them. And let them love you.

Love and let love.

It will set you free.

# How Many Libertarian Books Have You Read in the Last 90 Days?

"I've been a libertarian for eight years," said a high-tech friend. "But I'm still having trouble convincing people to become libertarians. Why?"

"I don't know," I said. "Let's take a look at what you're doing, and what you're *not* doing, and see whether we can figure it out."

We talked about who he was talking to and how he was talking to them. We dealt with a number of factors. Then I remembered something I had learned from America's foremost business philosopher, Jim Rohn.

Many years ago, Jim Rohn was a failure. And he couldn't figure out why. He worked hard. He was smart. And he didn't have any obvious vices.

Then he got lucky. He met Earl Shoaff. Earl was hardworking, smart... and really rich.

Mr. Shoaff hired Jim Rohn and taught him how to succeed. Jim Rohn was broke when he met Mr. Shoaff.

Six years later, Jim Rohn was a millionaire. Because he practiced what Mr. Shoaff taught him.

One of the first three questions that Earl Shoaff asked Jim Rohn was, "How many books have you read in the last 90 days?"

"Zero," said Jim Rohn.

And that was one critical reason why Jim Rohn was broke.

Mr. Shoaff's questions is a good one for us to ask ourselves.

How many libertarian books have you read in the last 90 days?

Not just glanced at. Not just skimmed. Not just started and

put away. How many libertarian books have you read — cover to cover — in the last 90 days?

When I asked my high-tech friend this question, he told me about the Web sites he'd visited. Which email newsletter lists he was on. Which think tanks he gave money to.

"Great," I said. "Now exactly how many libertarian books have you read — cover to cover — in the last 90 days?"

His face got red, and he said, "Zero."

"That's okay," I said. "Now how many libertarian books do you intend to read — cover to cover — in the next 90 days?"

"Well," he said, "I don't really know."

"Do you want to get the same results from your libertarian conversations in the next 90 days that you've gotten in the last 90 days?" I asked.

"No!" he responded.

"You can't build a house without the proper tools. That's what my writings, seminars, and tapes are designed to provide," I said. "But you *also* can't build a house without the proper building materials. Without cement. Without bricks. Without wood. Without glass for the windows. Without wiring or plumbing. Does this make sense?"

"Yeah. Like you say, this is a blinding flash of the obvious," he said.

"The building materials for constructing a libertarian understanding are the facts and principles of liberty. The insights and outlooks of liberty. The free-market economics. And small government," I said. "You've been trying to build an understanding without adequate building materials. Would you like to dramatically and positively change that, in only 90 days?"

"Absolutely."

Great news!

Reading libertarian books is not like the required reading you had to do in high school. No *Silas Marner*. No boring, symbolic novels. No textbooks written by a professor without a pulse.

Libertarian books range from short non-fiction (*The Law* by Frederic Bastiat) to long, challenging fiction (*Atlas Shrugged* by Ayn Rand). From economics to history. Current events. Theory. Science fiction. Libertarian books are a mosaic of different interests. A banquet of different tastes.

Don't let your public schooling get in the way of a real education. Because there's a libertarian book for you. A bookshelf you'll love and learn from.

Libertarian books are fun. So you're in for a real treat.

Here's what I suggested to my friend:

Buy three books: *The Great Libertarian Offer* by Harry Browne. The *Incredible Bread Machine* by Richard Grant. *Economics in One Lesson* by Henry Hazlitt.

Schedule 30 minutes each day for reading. The same time each day. While the road to hell is paved with good intentions, the road to heaven is paved with good habits.

I recommend your 30 minutes of reading first thing in the morning. No matter what comes up the rest of the day, your reading will not get pushed aside.

Read with an ink pen and a highlighter pen next to you. As you see points you want to remember, powerful paragraphs or compelling arguments, underline or highlight them.

If a page or a discussion puzzles you, or raises a question, write your question or reaction in the margin. John Locke said that we create ownership by "mixing our labor" with the material of the earth. We do not own a book until we mix our thought and labor with each page.

A well-read book is a well-marked book.

Your underlining, highlighting, and notes will increase your understanding and remembering.

When you finish reading the book, write the date on the inside cover. This way you'll know exactly when you read the book, even years later.

After 21 days, reread your notes, underlines, and highlights. This will refresh and strengthen what you learned.

I'd suggest you start with *The Great Libertarian Offer* by Harry Browne. Read it cover-to-cover, using the steps above. Then do the same with *The Incredible Bread Machine* by Richard Grant and *Economics in One Lesson* by Henry Hazlitt.

With only 30 minutes a day reading, you will become fluent with libertarian ideas and insights. You will have dozens of persuasive facts at your beck and call. To paraphrase Thomas Huxley, "An ugly statist theory, slain by a gang of beautiful libertarian facts."

With only 30 minutes a day reading, you will become more

confident and comfortable when discussing libertarianism.

Thirty minutes a day for only 90 days. A small difference that makes a huge difference.

My high-tech libertarian friend accepted the challenge. Will you?

How many libertarian books will you read — cover to cover — in the next 90 days?

# "If You Can Dream, and Not Make Dreams Your Master..."

"When we achieve freedom, the economy will flourish. Prosperity will be common. Poverty will be eradicated. I can hardly wait..." the speaker began. For the next 10 minutes, he spun out fantasies of how great freedom was going to be.

This dream was uplifting and inspiring.

"When we end the insane War on Drugs, when we end Drug Prohibition, drug abuse will be such a minor problem we probably won't even notice it," began another. For 15 minutes, he held court as libertarians imagined a world without Drug Prohibition.

This dream was pure oxygen for people suffocating from Big Government.

"In a self-regulating free-market economy, a laissez-faire economy, we'll see safer, cheaper, and better products. Ever-diminishing defects. Ever-shrinking flaws," began a third libertarian dreamer. He showered possibilities and likelihoods on the new libertarians who had come to hear him speak.

This dream was exhilarating.

Libertarian dreams point us true north.

They ignite our passions and inspire our minds.

They fuel our efforts.

They focus our energies.

We must begin with libertarian dreams. Or we'll never begin. But we cannot stop there.

Ayn Rand addressed this question in her story "Ideal." Two characters wondered why life was of no account. Who made it so?

"Those who cannot dream," said one.

"No. Those who can *only* dream," answered the other.

Those who cannot dream of liberty will never want it.

Those who can only dream of liberty will never seek it. They will fantasize and rhapsodize, but they will not act.

Does your dream of liberty inspire you to act? Does it motivate and activate you?

Does your dream of liberty whet your appetite to do? Does it make you hungry for a libertarian America in your lifetime?

Does it toss you into conversations about politics and economics? Does it make you feel like "I've got to tell everybody about these libertarian ideas"?

Does your dream excite and thrill you? Does it get your feet tapping and your heart pounding?

Does it set your soul afire? And do you burn so brightly you've just got to light the world for liberty?

Most people go through life without big, bold dreams. Share yours with them.

Without dreams, there's a hole in our hearts. We want dreams and we need them.

If necessity is the mother of invention, dreams are the father.

To invent a better America, we must dream liberty. A dream big enough to fill millions of hearts.

A dream big enough to inspire and activate.

We libertarians are dream merchants. When we talk with family or friends. When we offer a libertarian solution to a talk radio audience. When we write a letter to the editor. When we run for office.

We do not worship dreams. We work for our dreams. We do not serve dreams. Dreams serve us.

But only if we work to make them real. Only if we roll up our sleeves and act. And only if we keep working on them and for them.

We must love our dreams. Then we must live our dreams.

As Rudyard Kipling said, "If you can dream, and not make dreams your master..."

...We can bring our libertarian dream to life.

# Double Your Compassion and Your Money Back

Why do Americans tolerate government social programs that don't work?

Why are we willing to accept welfare programs that make people dependent?

Why do we condone a Social Security system that rips off young people while giving the elderly so little?

Because Americans are generous and compassionate people. Because we don't want to stand idly by while the weak and the frail suffer. Because we would rather endure flawed and wasteful government social programs than be indifferent to the needy.

We tolerate the programs because of the "good intentions" behind them.

Good intentions are not enough. We deserve good *results*. And good value for our money.

Compassion is not enough. We need a compassion that lifts people up. A compassion that returns them to self-reliance and self-respect.

Government social programs don't work. Government social programs hurt the people they seek to help. Government social programs create new problems. Government social programs squander billions of dollars. Government social programs divert money and energy from positive and productive efforts.

Government social programs. Government compassion. Motivated by the best of intentions. Fatally flawed. Crippling and destroying human lives.

This complacent compassion is unacceptable.

We need an *ambitious* compassion. A *demanding* compassion.

Do we care enough to consider a dramatically different way of helping the weak and frail and suffering?

Do we have intentions good enough and strong enough to insist on good results?

We must abandon government social programs. We must end government involvement in social matters. We must end government-run welfare... end tax-funded charity.

We must dramatically cut taxes, and let taxpayers decide which charities have earned their support.

We must move forward to the marketplace... the voluntary sector of the economy.

We must look to *The Tragedy of American Compassion* by Marvin Olasky and *Reclaiming the American Dream* by Richard C. Cornuelle. Or *Reinventing Civil Society* by David G. Green.

The marketplace delivers us ever-more-powerful computers at ever-lower prices. Government inflicts ever-more-expensive programs with ever-worsening results.

The marketplace succeeds because ineffective businesses can fail. Because better, more responsive businesses can replace them. So too, with a marketplace for compassion.

Free-market social programs combine the best of intentions with the best of systems. Competing to provide higher levels of compassion. With more of the social dollars reaching the beneficiaries.

Voluntary compassion seeks to give a hand *up*, not just a hand-out. Voluntary compassion seeks to restore self-reliance. Voluntary compassion transforms objects of charity into self-supporting individuals of dignity.

In the charity marketplace, social institutions must earn our support. They can't simply tax it like government does.

In the charity marketplace, social institutions must compete for our contributions. Must show us that they do more for the needy with every dollar we give them.

In the charity marketplace, social institutions must experiment and innovate. Must create dramatically better ways of meeting our social needs.

Social programs are too precious to leave in the clumsy hands of Big Government. They need the gentle hands of churches, charities, and communities. Freely giving and freely receiving. Do we care enough? Are we compassionate enough? Are our intentions good enough and true enough? Because only the voluntary sector, the gentle marketplace, can raise the level of genuine social service in America.

Here's our free-market charity guarantee: double your compassion *and* your money back!

# The One-Book Libertarian

I'm a book-aholic. I read over 100 books a year. Since I slowed down.

A lot of the orthodox, hard-core, old-style libertarians are book-aholics, too. Insatiable. Five, ten, or fifteen books a month. The ultra-marathoners of readers.

We read ourselves free. The complete works of Ludwig von Mises. Of Thomas Paine. Ayn Rand. Friedrich Hayek. Murray Rothbard. Frederic Bastiat. Henry Hazlitt.

So naturally, we expect new libertarians to read themselves free, too.

The problem?

Most new libertarians are *not* book-aholics. Some found their own way to liberty. Many were influenced and persuaded by Harry Browne's Presidential campaigns. Still others self-navigated to the Advocates' Web site, took the World's Smallest Political Quiz, read pages from the Web site, and realized that they were libertarians.

How do book-aholic libertarians try to persuade prospects to become libertarians? Books.

"Just read *Human Action* and you'll get it." "*Atlas Shrugged.* You've got to read *Atlas Shrugged.*" "*Man, Economy and State.* Just read it." "*The Road to Serfdom* changed my life. Wait until you sink your teeth into it."

But most prospects are *not* insatiable readers. Not voracious bibliophiles.

Neither are most people in this country. Most people have jobs, families, hobbies, friends, and even... personal lives.

The problem is that most of these people will not read

dozens of books on liberty. But, as Napoleon Hill said, "Every adversity contains the seed of an equal or greater benefit." Every problem is an opportunity.

Why?

Marginal utility.

If the prospects you're talking with read five, or 10, or 15 books a month, then every additional book has less impact on them. If you have a billion dollars in the bank, then receiving a million dollars has very little impact on you. If you don't have money in the bank, then receiving a million dollars may have a huge impact.

If you've read 1,000 books, then each additional book will have less impact. If you've only read five or ten books, than one book can change your life forever.

It's hard to persuade infrequent readers to read one book. But the payoff may be huge.

Because one good libertarian book can furnish their mind with the facts and insights of liberty.

Seek out infrequent readers. Convince them to read just one libertarian book.

But, as our friends in the martial arts warn us, we have "one encounter, one chance."

Make sure the "one encounter, one chance" libertarian book is interesting and readable.

Of all the books that I have given to infrequent readers, the following three have had the most impact on the most people:

1. *Why Government Doesn't Work* by Harry Browne.

2. *The Great Libertarian Offer* by Harry Browne.

3. *The Law* by Frederic Bastiat.

How do you get infrequent readers to read this one libertarian book?

Here's what I say: "John, I know you have a busy life. I know you don't have a lot of time left over for reading. But I just read a book that blew my mind. And I thought, John's just going to love this! John, could I ask you for one little-bitty favor? I bought this book for you and I'm glad to spend money on my friends. Would you promise me that you'll read this book cover to cover in the next couple of weeks? Would you do that as a personal favor to me?" (I make sure I get their agreement. Then I thank them.)

*Don't* do this with every libertarian book you like. *Don't* start dropping them off libertarian article after libertarian article... as a Chinese water torture test.

"One encounter, one chance." Make sure it's the *best* encounter, the *best* book, the *best* chance.

Because this libertarian book could change their life forever. This will be the book they discuss with their infrequent-reader friends. This will be the book they rely on to guide their political choices and actions. This will be the book they will recommend to all their friends and neighbors.

One-book libertarians will form the largest mass of the libertarian iceberg. They will have the largest influence on the largest number of people.

Look for infrequent readers. Wisely use your "one encounter, one chance." Turn them into one-book libertarians.

# The Karma of Conversation

Like attracts like.

Kindness begets kindness. Rudeness begets rudeness.

Mean people attract mean people. Friendly people attract friendly people.

Opposites repel. Abrasive people repel sensitive people. Argumentative people repel agreeable people.

We attract similars and repel opposites.

The karma of conversation: "As ye say, so shall ye reap." Want to know what someone's sowing? See what he's reaping.

Don't like what you're reaping? Sow what you want to reap.

In your conversations about libertarianism, what kind of people do you want to attract? Bright and eager to learn? Or stubborn and argumentative?

In your conversations about libertarianism, who do you want to draw in?

Agreeable or disagreeable people? Good-finders or fault-finders? Lovers or haters?

"As ye say, so shall ye reap."

Our attitudes and the way we treat people determine who we bring in and who we drive out. Forgivers or grudge-holders. Good neighbors or bad.

"As ye say, so shall ye reap."

What we say and how we say it makes all the difference.

Compare two questions:

- "What's your problem?"
- "What's troubling you?"

If you were having a bad day, which of the two would you rather hear?

"As ye say, so shall ye reap."

Life is an echo. It returns to us what we send out. Life is a mirror. It reflects what we present.

Reciprocation. We get what we give.

If our conversations are drenched in bitterness, frustration, and anger, who will we attract and who will we repel? Is this what you want?

If we attack and accuse, who will we attract and who will we repel?

"As ye say, so shall ye reap."

Does this mean that libertarians need to be back-slapping, glad-handing, grinning idiots? Not unless these are the kind of people we want to attract!

Why not be bright, courteous, and interested? Why not be articulate and well-informed? Why not be a living brochure for libertarianism?

The attitude, mood, and emotion we bring to the conversation are what we sow. And what we reap.

Give what you want to get. Sow what you want to reap.

Harness the karma of conversation.

Put it in the service of liberty.

# Do We Need Political DMZs?

What is abortion?

"Abortion is murder. Anyone who would have an abortion is a baby-killer. Shame on America for allowing the genocide of over one million abortions every single year," said the pro-life activist.

"Every woman has the right to chose. It's a woman's body, a woman's choice. Without legal abortion, hundreds of women would die from back-alley, coat-hanger butchers. We must keep abortion legal," answers the pro-choice activist.

What about immigration?

"America is a nation of immigrants. They are productive, responsible, hard-working members of society. They often take the jobs Americans refuse to take. Then they earn promotions or build their own businesses. America needs immigrants," said the advocate of open borders.

"America is being invaded by illegal aliens. They take advantage of free health care, public schooling, and welfare. They refuse to learn our language. They refuse to become true Americans," responds the advocate of closed borders.

The death penalty? Military intervention in other countries? School vouchers? The phony libertarian "purist" vs. "pragmatist" debate?

These issues are a free-fire zone for libertarians. There are good libertarians on each side. Our internal fights over these issues are often more brutal and ruthless than the fights we have with the backers of Big Government.

We need to turn these conflicts into a political DMZ. A political de-militarized zone. An area where civilians and non-combatants are welcome and safe.

An argument-free zone.

Why?

We've had no-win, endless arguments in these areas for years. The militant combatants refuse to withdraw their troops. Refuse to leave the battlefield. Refuse to beat their swords into plowshares.

The rest of us keep getting wounded and killed by their friendly fire. Our efforts are hindered and harmed by this ceaseless internal conflict.

As Ayn Rand observed, "The most vicious wars are civil wars."

We need a libertarian civil peace.

We need to take four steps.

**1. Notice what's happening in these libertarian political free-fire zones.**

What are the recurring, enduring conflicts? What does one side say? What does the other side say? What are the consequences and responses? Notice the ritual script that each side uses. Notice that neither side changes its mind. Notice that both sides look for new arguments to bolster and defend their positions.

**2. Declare a cease-fire.** Both sides need to stop shouting, stop shooting, and leave the battlefield. Both sides need to stop drawing non-combatants into their endless ideological wars. Need to stop making the rest of us feel frustrated, angry, and at the end of our ropes.

**3. Negotiate a truce.** Agree to disagree. Acknowledge that there are good libertarians on all sides of these issues. Agree that continued internal conflict divides us. Weakens us. Diverts our attention and energies from our true mission: to achieve individual liberty, personal responsibility, and small government.

**4. Create reminders for the truce.** We're flawed human beings. Sooner or later, someone's going to push our buttons. Someone's going to bring up abortion, immigration, the death penalty, or something else that will trigger our passions.

Here are a few reminders we may want to use:
- "We're in the political DMZ — let's agree to disagree."
- "Red light. We're turning this into a free-fire zone."

- "What if they gave a war and nobody came? This is a no-win war. I'm not coming."

Political DMZs do *not* resolve areas of conflict. They free us to work together where we *do* agree. Where we *can* cooperate. Where we *can* make progress.

If we *do* work together where we *can* work together, we can make government small.

And once we've achieved that, we can turn our energies to the more difficult problems.

# Libertarian Excitement is Contagious

"It is a sin to bore your fellow man," said legendary ad writer David Ogilvy. "You cannot bore people into buying."

Long, footnoted libertarian arguments cause the eyes of our listeners to glaze over. Breathing turns shallow. And the political coma soon ensues.

Obscure and trivial libertarian issues, presented in a monotone, delivered at great length... drive people away.

Libertarianism is the most exciting political philosophy on earth. It overthrows monarchies, frees slaves, and liberates women. It creates and sustains free minds and free markets. It breathes life into whole industries. It gives us lower prices, better service, and greater quality in the marketplace.

Libertarianism is the long-sought philosophers' stone — transforming poverty into prosperity. Making men and woman free and responsible.

Libertarianism pulses with passion.

Yet sometimes we fail to write and speak of it at the same high emotional pitch.

Where is our enthusiasm for free markets? Where is our passion for liberty?

### Excitement is the Secret to Selling Libertarianism

When car-maker Walter Chrysler was asked the secret of his success, he said, "The real secret is enthusiasm. Yes, more than enthusiasm, I would say excitement. I like to see sales people get excited. When they get excited, they get customers excited, and we get business."

Frank Bettger wrote, "During my 32 years of selling, I have

seen enthusiasm double and treble the income of dozens of salesmen. And I've seen the lack of it cause hundreds of salesmen to fail."

Writer Willa Cather said, "Every artist's secret is passion. It is an open secret and perfectly safe. Like heroism, it is inimitable in cheap materials."

Their passion fueled their careers. Their excitement and enthusiasm won them loyal customers and fans.

Imagine that excitement in every conversation you have about libertarianism. Because that excitement is infectious.

It makes libertarians and libertarianism contagious.

It keeps our ideas on the lips of people who hear them. And it makes libertarianism the subject that people talk about.

Would you like that?

Would you like libertarians to be so exciting and interesting, to so many people, that those people talk about it and keep talking about it with their friends and families?

That excitement inspires and motivates people to learn more about libertarianism. It almost guarantees that more people will hear about us and join us.

Patrick Henry's "Give me liberty or give me death" speech was drenched with passion. Saturated with excitement. He won the hearts and minds of all who heard. Tom Paine's *Common Sense* was burning with the love of liberty.

That is why these men won converts and why we won freedom. Excitement is contagious.

When we convey excitement about liberty, we're like the people Jack Kerouac wrote about in *On the Road:* "...the mad ones, the ones who are mad to live, mad to talk, mad to be saved, desirous of everything at the same time, the ones who never yawn or say a commonplace thing, but burn, burn, burn like fabulous yellow roman candles exploding like spiders across the stars and in the middle you see the blue center-light pop and everybody goes, 'Awww!'"

When people are exposed to this kind of excitement, they become libertarians.

### The First Step: Banish Boring and Tedious Topics
Sometimes people have questions about parts of libertarianism that simply don't interest us. Why not change the

subject to something you are interested in? For example:

"John, I can see you're interested in this issue, but I don't think I can be particularly helpful here. If I could find a book or an essay that deals with this concern, would you like to read it?"

"Jenny, I'm not familiar with the facts details of the issue you're raising. Would it be okay with you if I asked a few more knowledgeable libertarians about this and got some information for you? If I got it, would you read it?"

"Bill, that's a really good question. I don't know how to answer it. Knowing what you know about libertarianism, what do you think would be the best libertarian approach to this problem? What kind of voluntary solutions might be available? How might the marketplace deal with this issue?"

"Mary, I just don't know. Can we put this on the back burner, and talk about something I'm more familiar with?"

The master maxim: Stop having conversations about issues that leave you cold.

### The Second Step: Raise Your Level of Excitement

What excites you about libertarianism? What makes the hair on the back of your neck stand up? What makes your pulse race? That is the part of libertarianism that you can best communicate. That is the part of libertarianism you *must* communicate.

- Is it an issue, idea, or principle of libertarianism that races your motor?
- Is it a virtue or benefit of libertarianism that thrills you?
- Is it a unique or special impact that only libertarianism makes?
- Is it the hope or expectation of liberty in our lifetime?
- Or the chance to give a real legacy to your kids?

Ask your listeners what excites them about our libertarian ideas. What makes them feel hopeful or positive? What intrigues them? What arouses their curiosity? Why not let them bring excitement to the libertarian conversation?

Actively crank up your level of excitement when talking about libertarianism. Let yourself fall in love with it all over again. Take yourself back to that moment when you "got it."

And then bring back that excitement and hope and expectation.

If you want them to get it, you've got to give it.

If you want them to be excited about it, you must be excited about it.

Act as if. To be excited, act excited. To be enthusiastic, act enthusiastic. Wouldn't that be wooden or phony? No. The pathways that connect our feelings and our behavior run both ways. Being happy makes us smile. Smiling makes us happy. While it takes us a few moments to act ourselves into the feeling, when we finally switch it on, it sustains itself.

- Take a look at *Stress for Success* by sports psychologist James E. Loehr. You're going to love Chapter 5, "It's Showtime Every Day."
- Or dip into *Three Minute Therapy* by libertarian psychologist Dr. Michael Edelstein.
- Or *Wake Up and Live* by Dorothea Brande.

Dramatize and emphasize the best of libertarianism. Talk about the jazziest and juiciest parts. The things that make your mouth water. That make you weep with joy. As Michael Shurtleff wrote in *Audition*, "What good is truth if it's dull and boring? Exciting truths can be truthful, too. Learn to prefer those... truth isn't enough if it isn't dramatic." Why not encourage them to read some dramatic libertarian fiction?

- *Cash McCall* by Cameron Hawley.
- *The Moon is a Harsh Mistress* by Robert Heinlein.
- *Atlas Shrugged* by Ayn Rand.
- *And Then There Were None* by Eric Frank Russell.
- *The Night Thoreau Spent in Jail* by Lawrence and Lee.
- ...or your personal favorite.

### The Excitement Challenge

If you're not excited in your conversations about libertarianism, if you cannot generate excitement, you're having the wrong conversations.

Breathe life into your libertarian conversations. Passion and drama and aliveness. They will infuse your conversations with an intensity and power that wins people to liberty. Get excited about freedom.

Libertarian excitement is contagious.

# Are You Arguing Morality or Persuading?

Think back to the last few times you discussed libertarianism. Were you trying to show the other person why you're right? Or why he's wrong?

Did you bring out evidence and arguments to prove your points? Or disprove hers?

Did you frequently make moral judgments about government programs, actions, and policies? Did you render moral verdicts about the other person's ideas and beliefs?

Did you say that "coercion is immoral," "the initiation of force is evil," "welfare is wicked and wrong," "no one has a right to use force to achieve social ends," or "forbidding or compelling this is morally wrong"?

Sound familiar?

If it does, you're arguing morality.

Moral arguments rarely change people's minds.

Moral arguments often make people more resistant to libertarianism — or more opposed.

Put yourself in the other person's shoes. How would you feel if you were called "immoral" or "unethical"?

How would you react if someone said your beliefs are "morally wrong" or "evil"? How would you feel if someone morally condemned and vilified things you hold dear?

When we are attacked, our natural response is to defend ourselves.

Moral arguments are moral attacks. They trigger defense, not surrender. Escape, not submission.

"Moral lectures rarely change people's minds or behavior," observes psychologist Nathaniel Branden.

Self-righteous moralizing is neither attractive nor effective. Where moral condemnation fails, persuasion often succeeds. Persuasion opens the hearts and minds of many. Persuasion offers new choices and insights and outlooks. Persuasion shows the blessings and benefits of liberty. Persuasion shows how and where liberty will lift the back-breaking burdens of Big Government. Persuasion shows how and where liberty will be the dawn of breathtaking choices and opportunities. Persuasion offers the features, functions, and benefits of libertarianism. Persuasion is warm and gentle and appealing. Imagine how your family and friends and co-workers will respond to libertarian persuasion. Isn't that what you really want?

# Counterfeit Libertarianism

"I'm a moderate on economic issues," said the guest on *Politically Incorrect.* "But on the drug issue, I'm libertarian." "I'm an economic libertarian," wrote the columnist in *The Wall Street Journal.* "On tariffs and trade, I'm a libertarian," said the Democratic congressman.

We libertarians should feel flattered. No one forges bad paintings. No one counterfeits worthless currencies.

They fake, forge, and counterfeit the really good stuff.

Like "privatization." Robert Poole, the prime mover behind the Reason Foundation, has championed privatization for 30 years.

Government is involved in a number of activities that have nothing to do with defending our life, liberty, and property. Education. Charity. Medical insurance. Retirement programs. Housing programs. Just to name a few.

To privatize one of these activities is to take it out of the hands of government and turn it over to private enterprise. No government funding or involvement. Privately owned. Privately operated.

Robert Poole did an extraordinary job of promoting privatization. It proved itself. It got popular.

So the friends of Big Government started counterfeiting it.

They brag about "privatizing" prisons. They get "competitive bids" for "prison services." "We can lock up 12 drug offenders for 25% less than you'd pay if government owned and operated the prisons," they say.

They brag about "privatizing" education in some cities. They get "competitive bids" for "educational services." "We can teach kids the same things they learn in public schools for a lot less money," they say.

Perhaps they will soon brag that defense industries "privatize" the production of weapons of war.

"Privatization" means privately owned and operated. Private profit or loss. No government funding. No government involvement.

The friends of Big Government love to counterfeit privatization. A government contract is called "privatization."

Outsourcing Big Government activities is called "privatization." Business/government "partnerships" are called "privatization."

In privatization, there are more counterfeits than genuine articles. Like an art expert, Robert Poole will need to expose the fakes and authenticate the real stuff.

"Libertarianism" is attracting the fakers, forgers, and counterfeiters.

Why? Quality. Value. Performance. Libertarianism is the gold standard of political philosophies — 24-carat gold.

When someone is tolerant about something, he tries to cash in by calling his tolerance "libertarian."

When someone endorses a tiny fragment of free enterprise, he tries to pass his little piece of freedom as fully "libertarian."

When a person opposes a tax increase on his business — while supporting other tax increases that don't gore his ox — he may support his position by saying, "On this tax issue, I am a libertarian."

Sure. And when I eat a salad, I'm a vegetarian.

How do we protect the value of "libertarianism"?

1. Tell them what a libertarian is. "As you may know, the word 'libertarian' comes from the root word 'liberty.' 'Libertarian' means individual liberty and personal responsibility. This is only possible when government is small.

"Small government is a night watchman... a tiny institution... a skeleton crew doing only the bare essentials. Small government is limited to defending our lives, our liberty, and our property. A libertarian advances individual liberty by making government small."

2. Ask them the small government libertarian questions:

"Does your proposal reduce the size, power, authority, and resources of government? Does it make government smaller? Does it take us closer to small government?"

- Government power vs. individual liberty. A zero sum game. One grows at the expense of the other. When one advances, the other retreats. When one expands, the other shrinks.

- The only way to achieve and protect individual liberty is to shrink government. Reduce government. To be a libertarian is to make government small.

3. If the proposal takes a bite out of Big Government, tell them: "You're right. That is libertarian. It makes government smaller. It expands individual liberty."

4. If the proposal leaves Big Government as big, powerful, and tax-bloated as it is today, tell them: "Well, your proposal is tolerant. Permissive. That's good, but it's not really libertarian. It doesn't reduce the size, power, or resources of government. It doesn't make government smaller. Libertarian proposals make government small."

When government decreases, individual liberty increases. When government shrinks, individual freedom expands.

We can praise a good idea while pointing out that it is *not* libertarian.

Courtesy, civility, and kindness are praiseworthy, but they are not unique to libertarianism. And hopefully we will exhibit them when we point out that a person's idea is good, but not libertarian.

5. We must publicly and privately show people the difference between true libertarianism and counterfeit libertarianism. We must teach them how to tell the difference between genuine libertarianism and fake libertarianism.

We must point out the difference between real libertarianism and sham libertarianism.

We must expose the counterfeits — and get them out of circulation.

We must promote the authentic and original libertarianism — and get it into the widest possible circulation.

# You're Not Failing Enough

"Michael, it's easy for you to persuade people to become libertarians," said the voice over the phone. "I've tried, but I'm just not getting through. I'm not convincing anyone. Maybe I just don't have what it takes."

If only he knew how many times I've fallen flat on my face. How many times I've flubbed up and failed. How many times I still do.

"How will he know if I don't tell him?" I thought. So I told him. And told him. And told him.

"Would you like to know how I developed my persuasive skills?" I asked. "Would you like to know the secret of persuasion?"

"Yes, I would," he said.

Here's what I told him.

From 1975 through 1986, I had learned and discovered and invented a number of techniques of libertarian persuasion. But I hadn't mastered them.

Sometimes they worked and sometimes they didn't. I hadn't mastered these patterns of persuasion.

Then I stumbled upon a book entitled *A Touch of Wonder* by Arthur Gordon. One short chapter changed the way I looked at and learned persuasion. It solved my persuasion problem.

The chapter?

"On the Far Side of Failure," the story of Arthur Gordon's life-changing encounter with Thomas J. Watson, Sr., the founder of IBM. After the interview, Thomas Watson offered Arthur Gordon a job with IBM.

Arthur Gordon said he wanted to be a successful writer,

swallowed hard, then told Mr. Watson "about the years of writing failures, the endless rejection slips."

Thomas Watson replied, "It's not exactly my line, but would you like me to give you a formula for writing success? It's quite simple, really. Double your rate of failure."

Arthur Gordon was stunned.

"You're making a common mistake," said Thomas Watson. "You're thinking of failure as the enemy of success. But it isn't at all. Failure is a teacher — a harsh one, perhaps, but the best... You can be discouraged from failure — or you can learn from it. So go ahead and make mistakes. Make all you can. Because, remember, that's where you'll find success. On the far side of failure."

This is what Mary Kay Ash of Mary Kay Cosmetics meant when she said, "I failed my way to success."

Fail twice as often. Fail twice as fast.

Then analyze your failures. Analyze your successes.

Delete your failure patterns. Repeat your success patterns.

Double your rate of failure.

Frequently fail. Intelligently fail. What worked? What failed?

Fail differently. Learn from each new kind of failure.

You will trip over new ways to fail. Junk them.

You will stumble into successes. Practice them.

You will learn twice as fast. Twice as soon. Twice as much.

And you will find persuasion success on the far side of failure.

# You Can't Have What You Have to Have

Is there one person in your life that you "just have to" convince to become a libertarian?

A brother or sister, a co-worker or friend?

Someone important? Someone close to you?

Because that is the one person you'll probably fail to convince.

Why?

You can't have what you *have* to have.

When you desperately, urgently need someone's agreement, you scare them away.

When you've absolutely, positively got to win that contract, make that sale, make that deal... you'll crash and burn.

You'll push and pressure and plead. You'll try too hard.

They'll smell your fear, and refuse to negotiate or cooperate.

They'll sense your desperation, and hold out.

"Necessity never made a good bargain," says the proverb.

This is true in our business lives and our personal lives.

It is true in our libertarian outreach. In our efforts to persuade. You can't have what you have to have.

What can you do about this?

1. Stop trying to persuade the person you desperately yearn to persuade. You're wasting your time and his. You're making him more resistant to libertarianism. Leave him alone. Or let someone else take a crack at him.

2. Pick up a copy of *Three Minute Therapy* by libertarian psychologist Michael Edelstein. Use his ABC simple techniques to convince yourself that, while it would be better if you convince the person to become a libertarian, it's not catastrophic

or totally awful if you don't. Practice the *Three Minute Therapy* techniques and you will feel better *and* do better.

3. Spend time trying to persuade people you feel confident and comfortable with. People you do *not* desperately need to convince. People you'd like to persuade, rather than those you feel you absolutely must persuade.

You can't have what you have to have.

But you can have a lot of what you'd like. With your work, with your personal relationships, and with your persuasive encounters.

# The Song of Liberty

Communication is a song we sing.

Lyrics and music.

Sometimes we get the lyrics right — yet fail to connect.

The words are eloquent — but the music is wrong.

Sometimes it's not what you say. Nor how you phrase it.

It's the music.

How many times have we told our tale, shared our message, but failed to reach the person we were talking to?

Too many.

While there are many reasons we fail to communicate, often the problem is with our music, not the lyrics.

What is the music of communication?

It's the rhythm, the tempo, the beat, the speed. It's the volume, the timbre, the pitch.

If we're vocally "out of step" with the person we're talking with, we probably won't get through to them.

If we're out of sync with her, then she's also out of sync with us.

To effectively communicate, we must match and mirror the other's person's music.

Want to dramatically increase the effectiveness of your libertarian communication?

Match the other person's music. Talk at the same speed he talks. Speak at the same volume she does.

If he talks in short bursts, speak in short bursts. If she speaks in a specific cadence or rhythm, put your words to that music.

Pay attention to your results. Let them be your guide.

I know of several salespeople who have doubled and tripled their incomes just by consciously speaking at the same speed as their prospects.

I have taught this to formerly "dateless" friends — who now have active social lives.

I have seen this work with crisis counselors, emergency room nurses, and psychotherapists.

When we match, mirror, and pace their conversation music, we create rapport.

When we match, mirror, and pace their conversation music, they can finally hear our words.

It works in politics, in business, and in our social lives.

When you sing your lyrics to their music, you may just reach them with your song of liberty.

# Say Goodbye to Unintended Consequences

Actions have consequences. Intended and unintended. Government actions have consequences. Intended and unintended. Legislation, regulation, programs, and policies have consequences. Intended and unintended. Economists, political scientists, and social scientists often talk about the unintended consequences of a government policy or program. The side effects.

For example, Thomas Sowell showed that dramatically increased unemployment among African-Americans and other minorities was an unintended consequence of minimum wage laws.

Free-market economists identified and demonstrated the destructive unintended consequences of rent control, wage-price controls, licensing, tariffs, urban renewal, and government welfare programs — just to name a few.

Social scientists have researched, measured, documented, and communicated the destructive unintended consequences of government intervention in the marketplace.

And that, also, has an unintended consequence: that, in many political and economic and political matters, the concept and phrase "unintended consequences" has outlived its usefulness.

The new distinction? Foreseeable consequences or unforeseeable consequences. Predictable or unpredictable.

You don't have to drink the whole ocean to know it's salty.

You don't have to get drunk every night to know that you're headed for a hangover.

You don't have to pass a "living wage" bill — ("minimum wage" with better PR) — to know that it will throw African-Americans, Latinos, and other people of color out of work.

You don't have to pass new rent-control laws to know what the consequences will be.

We don't have to continue Drug Prohibition and the Drug War to find out the inevitable, foreseeable, predictable consequences. The destructive and tragic consequences. We already know.

We don't have to reinstitute alcohol Prohibition to know what the results will be. We already know.

The results are foreseeable. They are predictable.

In more and more areas of society and politics and the economy, there are fewer and fewer unforeseeable consequences.

There are fewer and fewer excuses for not knowing.

Say goodbye to "unintended consequences." Welcome and adopt "foreseeable consequences."

# Freedom Reborn

"We are losing," a libertarian activist said to me. "The USA Patriot Act. The Department of Homeland Security. The U.S. war with Iraq. The federal government making itself bigger and more powerful. Government is taking more and more of our liberties. It's hopeless."

I understand how he feels. If I dwell on what the federal government is doing, I feel discouraged. Sometimes even cynical.

But dwelling on the descending darkness does not bring back the light.

I agree that things look bad for liberty in America. I agree that government power is on the rise. I agree that things look bleak for the future.

This is why you and I must redouble our efforts to recruit, educate, and activate new libertarians.

Why we must reach out. Communicate. Persuade.

"The only thing necessary for the triumph of evil is for good men to do nothing," said Edmund Burke.

Why would good men and women do nothing?

Because we believe that nothing can be done. That our quest is impossible.

Because we believe that we are too weak to do what is needed.

Because we believe that there are too few of us to accomplish the task.

Because we allow the political news and Big Government propaganda to discourage us.

Because we discourage ourselves. And quit. Or make half-hearted efforts.

Because we discourage others. And talk them into abandoning their work for liberty.

Discouragement is easy. Quitting is easy. Surrendering is easy.

That easy path leads to tyranny.

I cannot promise victory for liberty. Not in our lifetime. Not in our children's.

I can promise you that liberty is worth working for.

I can promise you that liberty is worth the price.

I can promise you that others have endured far worse. And others have triumphed.

I can promise you that every person you bring into the libertarian movement increases our chances of victory.

I can promise you that I and thousands of other libertarians will work with you.

For freedom reborn.

# Take 100% Responsibility for Your Communications

It's easy to blame other people for not understanding what we said to them.

"That's not what I said." "You weren't paying attention." "You're twisting what I said."

"You're confused." "It's not that hard to understand. What's the matter with you?"

It's easy to blame other people when we don't grasp what they said to us.

"You're not being clear." "That's not what you said." "What's your point?"

We make ourselves right. We justify our communication choices and actions and patterns.

We make the other person wrong. We fault their listening and speaking.

We do this with our conversations at home and work. Privately and publicly.

And the people we're talking with are doing the same thing. They're blaming us. They're excusing themselves. They're making themselves right. And making us wrong.

"What we have here is a failure to communicate," said the antagonist in the film *Cool Hand Luke.*

This failure to communicate is the result of surrendering personal responsibility for our communications.

Do you want to become a powerful communicator?

Want to be two or three times as effective in every conversation you have — starting today?

Here's the secret: *Take 100% responsibility for your communications.*

There are two sides to this secret: speaking and listening.

**1. Speaking.** When speaking to another person, make yourself 100% responsible for them getting your message. Take 100% responsibility for communicating in such a way that they understand.

Take responsibility for setting up a good time and place to communicate. If the other person is tired or stressed out, set up a better time. If the place is too noisy or distracting, pick a better place.

Take responsibility for using words and examples that resonate with the other person's experience. Speak their language. Relate to their experience.

Take responsibility for getting frequent feedback from the other person. What are they getting? What are they not getting? What makes sense? What doesn't?

Take responsibility for varying and modifying and experimenting with what you're saying and how you're saying it — until they receive the message you're sending. Until they understand.

**2. Listening.** When listening to another person, make yourself 100% responsible for getting their point. Take 100% responsibility for understanding them.

Take total responsibility for the time and place of the conversation. Make sure that these factors are conducive for you hearing and grasping what the other person is telling you.

Take responsibility for giving feedback. For checking that you're hearing what they're saying. Ask questions. Confirm understanding.

Some people object to taking 100% responsibility by saying, "Michael, it's not fair. Why should I have to be 100% responsible for speaking and listening? Shouldn't the other person be responsible for his speaking and listening? Shouldn't he do his fair share?"

Here are a couple of responses I've used.

- "You're right. It's totally unfair. Are you willing to accept this unfairness — in exchange for becoming two or three times as effective in your conversations? Isn't that a small price to pay for being a powerful communicator?"
- "You can make other people wrong, blame them

for being unfair — and be an ineffective and frustrated communicator. Or you can take 100% responsibility, put your communication fate in your hands, and become a master communicator. Which do you choose?"

Whether it's fair or unfair, taking 100% responsibility for your communications will dramatically improve your communications. Personal. Business. Political.

Experiment with this for a week. What are your results? What's the same? What's different? What's worse? What's better?

Personal responsibility sets us free. In politics. In communication.

When you demand that other people be as committed to understanding and being understood, you're making yourself weak and ineffective.

When you blame the other person for miscommunication or misunderstanding, you're giving away your personal power.

Taking 100% responsibility for your communications puts you in the driver's seat. Gives you control. Makes you more effective and powerful.

When you take 100% responsibility for the other person understanding what you say...

When you take 100% responsibility for understanding what the other person says...

You will understand and be understood.

You will communicate.

# The Timing Difference

"The difference between salad and garbage is timing," noted Dan Kennedy.

The difference between powerful communication and wasting your breath is timing.

We can say the right words, in the right way, to the right person... and still fail to communicate.

If we have bad timing.

Powerful eloquence. A spellbinding story. A mesmerizing manner.

They can shrivel and die.

If we have bad timing.

How often is timing the weakest link in your communication chain?

How often is timing the strongest link?

Some communicators have mastered the art of timing. Of knowing when.

Here are a few of their secrets.

**1. They make timing a communication priority.** Just as airline pilots have a pre-flight checklist to make certain that all systems work, good communicators have a "pre-talk" mental checklist. Timing is high on this list.

**2. They identify factors that let them know that a person is receptive to the communication.** When? Where? In what circumstances? Before or after what? "Jack is always in a better mood after his workout." "Betty is eager to talk and listen right after dinner." "Steve likes to talk while he drives." "Sue loves conversations in the kitchen, while she's cooking."

**3. They ask others when and where they're open and**

**receptive.** They save the conversation for the right moments. **4. They ask friends and family about each other's conversational receptiveness.** "When and where is Jim most open to personal conversations?" "I notice that you are really good at resolving problems with Nina. Is there a time or a place that's worked really well for you and Nina?" **5. They watch and listen to good timers in action.** They model the other person's behavior. They try out and test the new behaviors. They make notes. Examine their results. They keep experimenting.

Good timing can dramatically enhance our conversations. Good timing can powerfully nurture our relationships. Good timing can change our lives.

# Stop Expressing Yourself!

"I've had enough of that guy's socialist garbage! I'm going to unload on him. When I'm through, he'll know what the free market is all about," said one libertarian.

"I'm fed up with this man's Big Government blather. He, and everybody within earshot, is going to know the truth. I'm going to straighten him out — once and for all," said another.

"Every time this nanny-state liberal opens his mouth, he demands more government. Him and his 'best and the brightest,' elitist, know-it-all liberal pals rant and rave for more government oversight, control, and power. I'm going to give him a piece of my mind that he won't soon forget," said a third.

Does some Big Government supporter push your buttons?

Does someone drive you to the boiling point?

Ever say, "That's the last straw!"

Then what do you do? What's your next move?

Here's what many people do. Here's what you may be tempted to do.

"Get it off your chest."

"Let him know exactly what you think."

"Give him a piece of your mind."

"Make him understand."

"Tell him a thing or two."

"Give him a dose of the truth."

This is a normal and natural reaction.

We express ourselves. Emotionally and intellectually. Fully and completely.

May I offer a suggestion?

Stop expressing yourself!

Start *communicating*.

There's a difference between a message being sent and that message being received.

A difference between writing and being read.

A difference between speaking and being heard.

A difference between expressing ourselves — and truly communicating.

When we're frustrated or excited by what someone is saying, we often leap into the fray. We express ourselves.

We make our points. Say what we want to say. Put our ideas on the table. Our attention is self-centered. On us and our ideas.

But true communication is a *partnership*. True communication requires empathy. Putting ourselves inside the other person's hopes and fears, beliefs and values, knowledge, and personal experience.

Ask yourself:

"How do I feel when someone 'tells me a thing or two'?"

"How do I react when someone 'gets in my face?'"

"How do I feel when another person 'unloads' on me?"

"How do I respond when someone publicly 'straightens me out' to everyone within earshot?"

"How do I feel when somebody 'gets something off his chest' — and puts it on mine?"

Because that's how your listener will feel and respond.

Is that what you really want?

True communication requires us to focus on what the other person wants and needs. To shape our message in such a way that it fits the other person's wants and needs.

True communication opens doors. It's a warm handshake, not a clinched fist.

True communication requires us to practice empathy. To see the world through her eyes. To hear it through his ears. To feel it through her emotions. To think it through his mind.

Communication demands much of us. But it pays off lavishly. For yourself. For others.

Stop expressing yourself!

Start communicating.

# One Way to Make Your Ideas Unforgettable

You remember *the* conversation. You finally got through to your friend. You showed him how and why Big Government programs don't work. And he got it!

Your friend was emotionally and mentally animated and engaged. He asked questions and made remarks that made it glaringly clear that he finally *got* libertarianism. That he finally understood and agreed.

Finally!

Two weeks later, you saw him again. And nothing you talked about remained. It had evaporated like desert's morning dew.

Why did the conversation fade? Why did the insights vanish? What happened?

Your powerful conversation got diluted and drowned in 1,400,000 words of communication in the last two weeks. Two solid weeks of other thoughts, other conversations, TV, radio, music, reading, writing, the Internet... all with a background of buzzing, booming, confusion. Over 1,400,000 words.

Information overload. An over-communicated society.

Little of your conversation survived this information flood. Little was remembered.

Forgotten ideas influence no one. Forgotten conversations change no one.

How do you make your ideas unforgettable?

Here's one way.

Marry your ideas to quotable quotes. Link your ideas to memorable aphorisms, provocative witticisms, and clever remarks.

Don't just say, "It's a bad time for libertarianism." Link it to:

"As Thomas Paine said, 'These are times that try men's souls.'"
Don't just say, "Higher taxes just mean that government will
waste more money." Link it to: "As P.J. O'Rourke said, 'Giving
money and power to government is like giving whiskey and
car keys to teenage boys.'"

Don't just say, "I know the libertarian movement is still
small." Link it to: "As Dante said, 'A great flame follows a little
spark.'"

Don't just say, "You're right; most of my libertarian ideas
came from other people through books and conversations."
Link it to: "As Edith Wharton wrote, 'There are two ways of
spreading light: to be the candle or the mirror that reflects it.'"

Link your libertarian point to a provocative Velcro quote.
Both will stick in the mind of the listener.

So where do you find unforgettable quotes?

Here are three of my favorite sources:

- *Peter's Quotations,* compiled by Lawrence J. Peter
- *Aphorisms,* selected by John Gross
- *The Most Brilliant Thoughts of All Time,* edited by
  John M. Shanahan

Dip into three or four pages at a time. Highlight, underline,
and make notes in the margins next to the quotes that trigger
your thoughts and feelings.

Dismiss the dull quotes. Court the lively. The inflammatory.
The dramatic. The clever. The deeply true. Those that speak
to you.

Dog-ear the pages. Bookmark. Use Post-it Notes.

When you find an unforgettable quote that makes your point,
put it to work.

In your email. Your conversations. Your talk radio call-ins.

Let your libertarian ideas hitch-hike a ride into the mind
with the unforgettable quote.

Let your unforgettable quote be the life preserver that keeps
your ideas afloat in the information flood.

Let your unforgettable quote make your libertarian
conversations unforgettable.

# The "Inevitability of Freedom": A Destructive Fallacy

"Freedom is inevitable," said John L. "Human nature, principles of economics, and the way the world works lead to freedom. Would you like to hear exactly why freedom is inevitable?"

"We can come back to that in a moment if you want," I said. "Could we clear up a few things first?"

"Sure," he said. "What would you like to clarify?"

"Let's start with the word 'inevitable,'" I said. "It means incapable of being evaded or avoided. It means inescapable, necessary, or certain. Gravity is inevitable. Do you believe that freedom is an inevitable as gravity?"

"Well, not exactly..." he said.

"Because human history is one long lesson of the *evitablility* of liberty," I interjected. "One rarely interrupted demonstration of who, what, when, where, how, and why individuals and societies can evade, avoid, escape, surrender, and forsake their freedom. Isn't this true?"

"Well, when you put it that way, I guess it is," he said.

"What other way can you put it?" I asked.

"I guess I mean it figuratively or metaphorically," he said. "That human nature and the facts and forces of reality favor freedom."

"A number of political, social, and religious movements proclaimed that destiny, the forces of history, or social momentum were on their side," I noted. "They preached their movement's inevitability. To their supporters. But even more so to their opponents. Would you like to hear why?"

"Yeah, I would."

"Movement leaders tried to convince followers that victory was inevitable — so the followers wouldn't give up," I said. "And to convince opponents that their movement's triumph was inevitable — so they would give up. Want to know why the 'victory is inevitable' propaganda backfired?"

"You've got me curious. Why did it backfire?" he asked.

"'Inevitability' tells people they are powerless. Unable to change or influence the outcome. Their efforts could not advance the outcome. Their enemies' actions couldn't stop it. 'Inevitability' tells people that their sweat and sacrifice and activism are impotent and meaningless. It makes people passive. It takes their activism out of gear — and leaves it idling."

"I still have good arguments for why freedom will triumph," John said.

"I imagine you have strong arguments for why freedom *can* triumph. For why it *should*. For why we'll be dramatically better off if it does. For why we can and should make certain choices and engage in certain actions to substantially increase our chances of attaining freedom," I said.

Then I said, "Please remember this: the 'inevitability of freedom' is both false and destructive. Believing in the 'inevitability of freedom' is a major obstacle to the possibility of freedom."

# Why is the Market
# for Liberty So Small?

Why haven't millions of Americans joined the libertarian movement?

Poll after poll shows that tens of millions of Americans express moderately libertarian to strongly libertarian opinions. Where are these invisible legions of libertarians?

Why aren't they signing up, enrolling, and getting involved with our efforts?

They want libertarianism. They want individual liberty, personal responsibility, and small government. They want what we are offering.

Yet they haven't come to us. They haven't called, written, emailed, or showed up on our doorsteps.

They haven't joined us.

There's nothing the matter with libertarianism. There's nothing the matter with them.

So... Why aren't there millions of Americans in the libertarian movement?

Why is the market for liberty so small?

Simple.

We understand free markets, but we don't market freedom.

A nineteenth-century businessman said, "Any fool can make soap, but it takes a clever man to sell it."

Seminal libertarians have conceived and produced libertarianism's "product line." John Locke, Thomas Paine, Adam Smith, Ayn Rand, Rose Wilder Lane, Isabel Patterson, Ludwig von Mises, Leonard Read, Milton Friedman, Robert Nozick, Harry Browne, and dozens of other brilliant theorists and popularizers, vital thinkers and writers and speakers have made what we offer America and the world.

Now it is time to market liberty. To sell liberty to the tens of millions of prospective freedom customers.

We face the same challenge that every business in America faces: to reach, appeal to, and earn the business of new customers. To create brand loyalty and company loyalty. To instill such excitement and enthusiasm that they promote our product and company to their family, friends, and co-workers.

By providing them with exactly what they want and need, we develop unshakeable customer loyalty. And repeat business.

But it starts with marketing and selling libertarianism. This is the indispensable key to business success — and libertarian political success.

This is why the Advocates for Self-Government was founded. This is why I have worked over 27 years developing and testing and perfecting my "Art of Libertarian Persuasion" seminars.

This is why I write the "Persuasion Power Points" column for the Advocates' *Liberator Online* email newsletter.

The libertarian movement needs your help to effectively market liberty.

We need your best efforts and skills in selling freedom to America.

Join us, use the best persuasion tools and training, and 10 years from now, everyone in America will ask:

How on Earth did the libertarian movement in America get so big, so effective, so fast?

# The Unsettling Question
# Libertarians Almost Never Ask

The question: "If every libertarian in America did exactly what you did to advance liberty in the last 30 days — no more and no less — what would the measurable results be?"

How many people would have heard our libertarian message for the first time ever?

How many new libertarians would there be?

How many new activists would we have?

How many new supporters and donors would the libertarian movement have?

Look closely at what you did during the last 30 days.

Maybe you went to a libertarian meeting. If every libertarian in America went to the same kind of meeting, what would the measurable results be?

Perhaps you read a libertarian book or publication or email newsletter. If every libertarian in America read the same material, what would the measurable consequences be?

Suppose you discussed or debated libertarianism with a conservative or liberal. If every libertarian in America had the same discussion or debate, what would the quantifiable results be?

How many new libertarians? New activists? New supporters and donors?

You may have engaged in libertarian political activism or campaigning.

If every single libertarian in America put in the same amount of time, energy and money as you did in the last 30 days, which laws, regulations, mandates, or restrictions would be reduced or repealed?

Which taxes, government fees, and other government burdens would be reduced or removed?

How much measurable libertarian progress would we have today, if every libertarian in America gave exactly what you gave and did exactly what you did during the last 30 days?

"The unexamined life is not worth living," said Socrates.

Sometimes it's uncomfortable or disturbing to discover what we're really doing with our lives. Where we're actually putting our time and money. What's important enough to do something about.

Actions have consequences. Libertarian actions have libertarian consequences.

Wishes and hopes and good intentions accomplish nothing — unless they blossom into action.

Individual rights mean nothing — unless we establish them through action.

Do you want to just hope and talk about liberty? Or do you really want to be free?

Inaction inspires no one.

Action inspires many. Progress inspires more. Success inspires most.

Your actions demonstrate what's really important to you. Your actions proclaim your true values.

Act to advance your libertarian values for the next 30 days. You don't have to do something superhuman or extraordinary. Just plan a doable amount of productive libertarian activism during the next 30 days.

Don't make a resolution to do it. Plan to do it. Then do it.

Don't announce you're going to do it. Just do it.

Don't demand that others do it. Just do it.

You may be astonished by the results. And by the activism they inspire.

One last question:

"If every libertarian in America does exactly what you do to advance liberty in the *next* 30 days — no more and no less — what will the measurable results be?"

# AFTERWORD

## BY SHARON HARRIS

When I first encountered libertarian ideas in the late 1960s, I was excited. These ideas, I was convinced, could change the world. If only more people knew of them!

I wanted to do everything I could to share these ideas with others. To win their support and enlist them in the great cause of liberty.

Unfortunately, I didn't know the first thing about how to *communicate* those ideas. I blush today when I think about some of the awful errors I made — errors that turned many, many people off to libertarianism instead of persuading them to embrace libertarianism.

In fact, I made just about every communication error imaginable.

Even worse, I wasn't alone. Many other libertarians were making similar mistakes — attempting to spread our ideas in ineffective, self-defeating ways that often won us more opponents than converts.

Michael Cloud was one of the first people to see this — and to try to do something about it. He realized that if the liberty movement was to succeed, it was urgent that libertarians learn and master the very best ways to turn people on — not off — to our ideas.

Michael began to systematically explore how to do this. In the 1970s he launched a series of communication workshops that revolutionized the libertarian movement (as his current seminars continue to do today). In 1987 he put some of his very best communication insights into "The Essence of Political Persuasion," an acclaimed audio learning course still very